Contents

Dedicated to my wife Yvonne for her loyalty and support, which have given me confidence to continue with research and writing over a period of twenty years.

I would like to thank the following people and organisations:

Grace Cory, for all her help each month in ensuring articles and accompanying photographs were finished and ready for printing in the *'North Cornwall Advertiser'*. Maureen Tooze, Curator of Bodmin Town Museum, for access to the *'Cornish Guardian'* collection and permission to copy photographs. Dudley Prout; Pat Munn, *Cornish Bard and historian*; Jim Edwards, *Launceston local historian* and Charlie David, *North Cornwall District Council* for useful information and discussion. The helpful staff at Bodmin Library. The Cornish studies Library, Redruth, for permission to use photographs from the *'Ellis Collection"* and the Copyright and collection holders who have allowed the use of their photographs, including the Tyn-y-Coed, Hotel, Capel Curig; Glen Dimplex Home Appliances, Ltd. *(Belling & Co. Ltd.)* and BRB (Residuary) Ltd. *(Clapham Railway Museum)*. Bill and Janet Johnson, for their enthusiasm and many hours of committed hard work in bringing this book to fruition. Finally, thank you to those who have contributed information along the way.

Special thanks to Bodmin Town Museum colleagues for their warm friendship and continued belief in the success of the Museum.

P J C Davies, October, 2006

Bodmin Beacon

Bodmin Beacon at 532 feet above sea level, together with the 144 feet high Gilbert Monument, ensures the town is not lost in our Cornish landscape.

On a clear day we have a wonderful panorama – Helman Tor, Castle-an-Dinas, Stepper Point, River Camel estuary, Delabole Quarry, Rough Tor, Brown Willy, together with a wide sweep of Bodmin Moor to Caradon Hill, Dartmoor and the South coast.

The combined height of Beacon and monument at 676 feet has enabled steeplejack David Dawson to locate 18 parish churches: Nanstallon, Withiel, St Wenn, Roche, St Dennis, St Mabyn, St Endellion, St Minver, Helland, St Breward, Delabole, St Cleer, Rame Head, Lansallos, Braddock, Lanhydrock (through the trees in winter only), Lanlivery and Bodmin. The late Mr Gerald Thomas supplied the above information which often led to quite a debate when walking on the Beacon.

It was thought that the Beacon was formerly part of a large holding belonging to the Priory and on dissolution of the monastery the lands became vested in the local Borough Council. In 1974 the Beacon land was transferred to the North Cornwall District Council when Bodmin lost its borough status and then under the Local Authorities Act 1977 it was transferred to Bodmin Town Council.

In the early part of the last century the churches were falling into disrepair and the council found themselves responsible. In 1815 a bill was brought before parliament to empower the mayor and burgess of Bodmin to enclose and sell common land for the purpose of repairing the church and providing a new market house. The project for the enclosure of the common land was so unpopular among townspeople that it caused considerable rioting and disturbance, the militia was called in and that portion of the bill was withdrawn.

There was a reference to the Lord of the Manor of Bodmin, who is believed to have been a Mr Marks of Lostwithiel. It is understood that the office carried no emolument of any kind, but had the right to hunt hares on the Beacon. This ancient title ceased to exist in 1925. The council resisted a challenge to the Beacon skyline in 1935, when the Electric Lighting and Power Company had a request to take lines across turned down. That year the borough changed over from the DC to AC current.

The monument was erected in 1857 at a cost of £1,500 in memory of Sir Walter Raleigh Gilbert, a descendant of Sir Walter Raleigh. Gilbert was born in Bodmin in 1785 and at the age of 15 he joined the British Army as a cadet and served in the Bengal Infantry, India. During his army career Gilbert fought in the Sikh Wars of 1845 and had a distinguished military service. He received a Baronetcy from Queen Victoria in 1851.

Plans of the monument were given to Bodmin Borough Council by Robert Pease, solicitor of Lostwithiel. These plans, drawn to scale, are detailed and are of two elevations, to the north and west, and every course is shown. There are full details of the base and the eight courses which constitute it, plus the number of 'through stones' which come at the 13th, 22nd, 31st, 42nd, 49th and 58th courses of the shaft. Iron bars are situated at the 7th course of the shaft. The base is 31 feet 3 inches in height, the shaft 98 feet and the apex 14 feet 9 inches. The work was completed to tender by a Helston builder, Thomas Eva and Bodmin architect Joseph Pascoe was commissioned to supervise the construction.

Mr John Rowe of Town Wall worked on the monument during its construction, which is hollow for a great part, and claimed he was the last person to leave the inside before the final block was put in to seal it. Incidentally, this final block is the one with the word 'Born' inscribed on it.

When asked to state an opinion in 1933 on the condition of the monument, Messrs Dawson & Son, steeplejacks, thought the huge granite blocks too large for the class of work. With the natural swaying of the obelisk in a gale, there is no elasticity or 'give' in the granite. Because it is hollow, the monument swings 3 feet in strong winds. Some monuments are larger than Bodmin's but are round and therefore do not receive so much buffeting.

With reference to the laying of the foundation stone it has been said, "there were not many people there, it was a wet morning. The Mayor Mr Gilbert Hamley, uncle of Sir Walter Raleigh Gilbert laid the stone, the corporation were there, but not many townspeople."

The town did at one time lay out the Beacon as a playing field and put a pitch there for cricket, but had problems with certain townsfolk who galloped horses across it.

'Q' Quiller-Couch recalls the days he played rugby when there were twenty-a-side. He refers to "those wild days when he played on the Bodmin Beacon where the turf was less than three inches thick and the sub soil was granite. After being manhandled one knew who one was, but one's parents were lucky if they did."

Wrestling tournaments were held in the great wrestling ring near to the monument and many famous wrestlers were seen in action there. In 1912 crowds of people assembled on the Beacon to watch the 'First Flying Man at Bodmin' - the French aviator M Salimet. His aircraft variously described as an aeroplane, an airship and a flying machine with engine.

1994 saw the creation of a Local Nature Reserve, bringing in the district council's fields adjoining the Beacon open space, giving almost 72 acres in total. Today the work continues to encourage a diversity of wildlife, with a number of fields managed as hay meadows. Over 18,000 trees, mainly broadleaf, have been planted and a community woodland is developing. It was stated in the 19th century that Bodmin Beacon was "a favourite public promenade in fine weather." The same could be said today.

Bodmin Priory: 1,500 years of Cornish history wrapped up in house and grounds. From monks to money men.

When we park our car in Priory Car Park, many of us cannot help but admire the beautiful surroundings. Through this article we can learn the history of the house and grounds.

September 1928 saw the auction of Priory House and its grounds. Let us then pick up a copy of the prospectus and learn of the history of Bodmin Priory.

A representative of Messrs Knight, Frank and Rutley, the well known London Auctioneers, on Saturday 8th September 1928, at the Royal Hotel, Bodmin, offered at auction the Priory, Bodmin, by direction of the representatives of the late Mrs Gilbert.

The Georgian residence provides the following accommodation: entrance hall, boudoir, dining and drawing rooms, six bed and dressing rooms, sitting room and library, fitted bathroom, domestic offices. Company's water and gas supplies; also a private gravitation water supply on the estate from St Petroc's Well. Set of farm buildings and several enclosures of fertile accommodation grassland.

Out premises include knife house, wood store, wash house with copper, old brew house, two division cellars with loft over, apple room, old laundry, potato room, coal and wine cellars and two bay open sheds and coke house in the yard.

The stabling and garage comprise four loose boxes, two stalls with loft over, coach house or garage for two cars and harness room.

The grounds have the great attraction of maturity and are charmingly timbered.

From the south side of the residence: a pleasure lawn (under which the foundations of the chapel were discovered within recent years) stretches to the fringes of 'the Prior's Pool' or the fish ponds (believed to be the old stew ponds of the monks) which are stocked with rainbow and brown trout and carp and is fed by a stream. The banks and island are clothed with masses of rhododendrons, azaleas and bamboos and bordered by beeches, sycamores and oaks. On the east side, occupying a sheltered position is the formal garden (under which some of the priory cellars are said to exist) consisting of four sets of box bordered flower beds, arranged in geometrical designs and having a pergola in the centre of one set. A rockery, built of the original Priory carved stone work and rose garden. Unusual features comprise six bone-edge flower beds and three stone coffins used as water troughs. The glass house comprise a three division green house, one division of which is devoted to peaches and nectarines with stoke hole and boiler and fernery containing the old Priory granite font, gargoyles and pieces of carved stone work and a range of cold frames. In addition there is a dove house, galvanised iron poultry house, a brick built and slated bee house and a potting shed.

The kitchen garden, on which it is believed the Priory Church stood, is well stocked with wall cherry and pear trees, raspberry, gooseberry and currant cage, fig trees and asparagus beds.

The sporting facilities are exceptionally good and include hunting with the North and East Cornwall packs of fox hounds and with the Fowey Harriers. Golf can be played at the Royal Cornwall and St Enodoc Golf Links, two and twelve miles distant respectively. Trout fishing can be enjoyed in the Rivers Camel and Fowey, each within a distance of about three miles. There is the Royal Fowey Yacht Club at Fowey.

Having delivered full details of the property, grounds and history, the auctioneer expressed the hope that there was someone among the audience, public spirited enough to purchase the estate and present a portion of it to the county town. He declared that there was no property in Bodmin that was so ripe for development as was that which was that day being offered. He also alluded to the wonderful new approach to the town which could be made through it and to its value for building development.

The property, which comprises the comfortable Georgian residence and the farm buildings and 34 acres of pasture land, was first offered in one lot. For this, a bid of £4,000 was given, which rose to £5,600, when the auctioneer announced that it must be withdrawn at that figure.

Bidding for the residence, with its stabling, grounds, gardens and fishponds, started at £1,000 and, by bids of £100, raised quickly to £2,000, at which figure Messrs Coodes and Gifford (St Austell) purchased it for a client who, we understand, is a member of the Gilbert family.

The Priory House remained in the occupation of this family until shortly before the Second World War during which it was used as a billet for the ATS. A vacant period after the war followed until it was purchased in 1949 by the Bodmin Borough Council, for Municipal Offices, from Lady Newbolt, a descendant of the Gilbert family.

The local newspaper reported as follows:

"Bodmin and Priory Estate - Last Night's Decision of Town Council

- Playing Fields and War Memorial"

After two years of Negotiations and discussions, Bodmin Borough Council last evening, by a unanimous vote, decided to purchase the Priory Estate for conversion into a recreation centre for the townspeople and a public memorial of the 1939-45 war.

Alderman H G Kinsman moved acceptance of the recommendation of the Parks Committee, that the Council should take steps to complete the purchase of the estate at an early date, so that development could be commenced and the adoption of the scheme outlined in their report. Supporting the purchase, Mr A J Taper said the people in Bodmin were suffering the consequences of their forefathers' lack of foresight. If they bought the estate, they would have something to pass on to the next generation.

Mr Hore thought the question of a town War Memorial had been lost sight of. It had been generally accepted by the townspeople that if the Priory Estate was purchased it would be the town War Memorial. That was a point that would commend itself to the people. Alderman Kinsman agreed that it would be a wonderful opportunity for the many social organisations and voluntary workers in Bodmin to set up something for the benefit of the living as a memorial to those who died in the last war. The Parks Committee would do all they could to raise money by voluntary effort.

Remarking that he had always been a strong supporter of the purchase, Mr C Bricknell said they sometimes had to take risks and he thought the purchase of the estate a good risk for the Council to take. "I think the next generation will call this Council 'blessed' for what we are to do tonight," he added.

Mr H Taylor, Miss J A Foster and Mr G J Smith also spoke in support and the members present voted unanimously for the purchase of the estate and its development.

Referring to the visit of Sir Noel Curtis-Bennett, the Chairman of the National Playing Fields Association, to Bodmin last week, the Mayor, Mr W Bound, said Sir Noel told them that immediately the children's corner was started the association would make a special grant towards its cost. He also said that we should have the model playing field of the West of England; something of which we should be proud and the people of Bodmin would be proud and be ever grateful to the Council for their foresight.

11

The purchase of Priory House and Estate did not complete its passage through to completion without encountering some troubled waters, but such was the pride of the Bodmin Borough Mayor, Walter Bound, in the purchase of Priory House and grounds that part of the inscription on his headstone within Berry Tower Graveyard reads "By his casting vote as Mayor, the Priory Estate was secured for the people of Bodmin for all time."

Local government reorganisation took place in 1974, with North Cornwall District Council being created. Priory House became the administration offices of the new authority, with the grounds owned and managed by Bodmin Town Council. October 1992 saw the District Council move to newly built premises at Higher Trenant, Wadebridge and Cornwall County Council acquired the Priory House, today housing Social Services.

Historical notes

The Priory takes its name from the ancient Priory of St Petroc, stones and relics from which lend a special charm and interest to its grounds.

Towards the close of the fifth century, Guron founded a hermit's cell in the then thickly wooded upper valley of the River Camel. In about the year 518, four holy men from Wales, Petroc, Credanus, Medanus and Dracunus, landed in the estuary of the Camel, and came to him.

Guron resigned his cell to Petroc, who after a sojourn in Ireland, returned to live there and prevailed upon King Constantine II of Cornwall to grant him land for a monastery. He died in the summer of 564, before the building was complete and on his canonisation his remains became its most treasured possession and a goal of pilgrimage. Bod-manach or Bod-manniu, "the monks' dwelling" as the foundation was called, is said by some authorities to have given rise to the name of Bodmin. King Athelstan enlarged the place in about 926.

Great tribulation fell upon this community in the year 1177, shortly after the Epiphany, when one of their number was found to have stolen the bones of St Petroc and fled with them to the abbey of St Mevennus in Brittany. Roger, Prior of Bodmin sought the help of King Henry II, and through his intervention the relic was finally restored to the Priory enclosed in an ivory casket.

Except for a storm which wrought havoc in 1339, and for visitations of the plague, the life of the Priory thereafter appears to have been uneventful until the general dissolution of religious houses. It was ceded by the prior, Thomas Wandsworth, on 27th February 1538; its land comprised about 110 acres and its income £270. The site and lands were sold by the Crown to Thomas Sternhold, groom of the robes to Henry VIII. By 1567 they had passed to Nicholas Pescod and William Pydderley, who in that year sold them to John Rashleigh, merchant of Fowey.

The immediate site of the Priory was bought from the Rashleigh family by William Pennington, whose niece, Nancy, carried it in marriage to Major Walter Raleigh Gilbert, Deputy Lieutenant of the County of Cornwall, 1792, from whom it descended to a nephew of the same name, and in whose family it remains to the present day.

The Priory House was completely rebuilt under the conditions of a lease during the years 1766-1772. The terms being that there should be erected "in a strong and substantial manner a good handsome dwelling house with proper conveniences at a cost of not less than £800."

The property passed into the Gilbert family whose ancestors include the Elizabethan, Sir Humphrey Gilbert, half brother of Sir Walter Raleigh.

A connection between the Borough and the Gilbert family is the 'Gilbert Monument' a 144 feet obelisk, erected in the years 1856-1857 by subscription at a cost of £1,500 to Sir Walter Raleigh Gilbert who died in 1853 after noted service in India and elsewhere. The Borough Council, at a meeting on 24th May 1854, undertook that the whole area of the Beacon should be kept unenclosed for the use and recreation of the public.

Bodmin Methodist Church, 2006

©WHJ

For John Wesley - moorland weather – Tried the Patience of a Saint!

As the curfew bell tolled out its message on the Monday evening of the 19th August, 1743, little did the bell ringer, high up in the church tower of St Petroc's realise that as he laboured away he was helping to advance Methodism in Bodmin.

Let us here refer to John Wesley's journal of that particular day: "We rode forward. About sunset we were in the middle of the great pathless moor beyond Launceston. About eight we were, got quite out of our way, but we had not gone far before we heard the Bodmin Bell (Curfew Bell). Directed by this, we turned to the left, and came to the town before nine".

This can be confirmed in the words of John Nelson, one of the three companions who accompanied John Wesley on his first passage into Cornwall: 'Mr Downes and I had but one horse, so we rode by turns ... we generally set out before Mr Wesley and Mr Shepherd. One day, having travelled twenty miles without baiting, we came to a village (Trewint) and enquired for an inn; but the people told us there was none in the town, nor any on our roads within twelve Cornish miles: then I said, "Come Brother Downes, we must live by faith". When he had stood a while, I said, "let us go to yonder house, where the stone porch is, and ask for something": so we did, and the woman said, "we have bread, butter, and milk, and good hay for your horse." When we had refreshed ourselves I gave the woman a shilling; but she said she did not desire anything; I said "I insist upon it." We got to Bodmin that night; but it was late before Mr Wesley and Mr Shepherd arrived, having lost the path on the twelve mile common and found the way again by the sound of bells.'

Poor Wesley, his comments about Bodmin were often less than flattering, but perhaps the rough journey over the moor when at this period, the ancient highway we now know as the A30, was often overgrown and tangled with a mass of cattle tracks, and the weather he always seemed to encounter, would, we say, try the patience of a saint. He rode from Newbury Berkshire Monday April 2nd, 1744. On arriving at Launceston he found conditions vastly different. His journal records; "the hills were covered with snow as in the depths of winter. About two we came to Trewint, wet and weary enough, battered by rain and hail for some hours. I preached in the evening to many more than the house would contain ... In the morning Digory Isbell undertook to pilot us over the great moor, all the path being covered by snow, which in many places was driven together, too deep for horse or man to pass.

The hail followed us for the first seven miles; we had then a fair but exceeding sharp day."

1769 August 30th, "We had incessant rain, however reached Bodmin about eight." 1774 August 31st, "The rain, with violent wind, attended us all the way to Bodmin. A little company are at length united here. At their request I preached at the Town Hall (Guildhall) the most dreary one I ever saw! to a mixed congregation of rich and poor. All behaved well; and who knows but some good may be done at poor old Bodmin."

The village of St Lawrence close to Bodmin fared no better; in 1751 he visited, "A little, ugly, dirty village, eminent for nothing but a hospital for lepers."

Bodmin was perhaps a resting point for Wesley after crossing the moor, for it was in the west of the Duchy with its high mining population that he found his preaching was received. But Methodism had taken root in the town, and by 1797 permission was granted, only the second at the time in Cornwall to have its own sacrament.

Mr John Pethybridge in a review reported in the 'Bodmin Guardian' of May 1940, said he thought the first preaching place to have been in Chapel Lane, but in 1839 there was a need for a larger chapel, and when the plans were unveiled and the size of the building realised, the people of Bodmin asked the question, "What are the Methodists going to do, build a cathedral?" It was called the Centenary Chapel because it was commenced in 1839 and marked the centenary of Methodism. He believed the actual cost was about £1,600 and was opened on Thursday May 7th, 1840. In the 1880s a suggestion was put forward that the chapel be put on a level with the street, this did not carry favour, but work was started on building the Sunday school Assembly rooms along side the alterations to the Chapel costing, all told, Mr Pethybridge thought, about £5,000, with the reopening in 1886.

The late 20th century has seen the coming together of the chapels under one roof. Bodmin in 1990 saw a splendid civic service to mark 150 years, Mr Crocker preached an admirable sermon and to partly echo Wesley: he preached to rich and poor! All behaved well and who knows but some good may have been done.

I do recommend a visit to Trewint and visit Isbell cottage, it is brown-signed off the A30. On sale at the cottage is a little book called 'Trewint' by Thomas Shaw well worthy of purchase.

Friary Ruins as a "lion" of the place

It is a great pity that several fine old buildings, either noted for their size, historic interest, or beauty, should have been destroyed from time to time, in Bodmin. There should have been a refusal on the part of the Borough Council to have allowed any further sweeping away of such buildings, whenever possible.

The Friary Church, which stood where the present Assize Hall and the Public Rooms now stand, was only one foot shorter than St Petroc's Church, Bodmin; being 150 feet long and 60 feet high, according to the statements to be found in the Kelly's Directory. The width is not given. This building (reports Kelly's Directory) was partially destroyed in 1837 to make room for the Assize Hall; having been itself previously used as an Assize Court. No doubt this building had been for a long time in a ruinous condition, and the mere shell of its former splendour, but even if it had been kept as a ruin, with ivy on the walls and carefully kept turf on the ground, it would have been an object of interest and beauty. The Assize Hall should have been built elsewhere. Henry VIII robbed this church and the buildings connected to it; and sold what was not his to the Vyvyan family in 1546, who sold this property to the Corporation of Bodmin in 1566. The Gatehouse (today Michael Cornelius Jewellers) ought to have been kept in the state discovered in the alterations a few years ago, when a good arched entrance and niche were found under the plastered front. The House of Grey, or Franciscan friars, which stood at Mount Folly, was certainly in existence in 1253 but the circumstances of its foundation are uncertain, although the Plantagenets, Earls of Cornwall and one John de London, a merchant, appeared to have shared in establishing it. Within its precincts were buried Sir Hugh Peverel, Kt. and Sir Thomas Peverel, Kt., both benefactors of the Friary. If only the Assize Hall and the Public Rooms could have been built in some other part of Bodmin, there would have been these Friary ruins as a "lion" of the place. There is plenty of ground in and near Bodmin for buildings. Bodmin is not like some huge city, where ground is scarce anywhere near the centre of the place. Again, if the Priory ruins had been allowed to remain and the present dwelling house, known by that name, had been built further up the valley towards Priors Barn, another fine old ruin would have been an attraction to visitors.

The fine old porch in Pool Street has been quite recently destroyed, the most interesting part (the porch, with room over) being removed and a passage cut through to a yard behind. The pavement was wide enough without removing the projecting porch and some other way of getting to the

BTM

Tudor porch house, Pool Street (demolished ca. 1900)

yard could surely have been made.

The above article was the strongly held opinion of a writer over one hundred years ago. But without a doubt the Friary Church of St Nicholas was a magnificent building, eminent travellers and historians of that period spoke of the hammer-beam roof as only second to that of Westminster Hall, rising to a height of 60 feet.

The Friary occupied around five and a half acres stretching back beyond the old Assize Court building. The Franciscan/Grey Friars could be regarded as the Salvation Army of their time, working with the very poor and the infirm.

The Reverend W Iago records the final moments of the Church destroyed in 1891: *A strong rope, a noose of iron chain, with powerful hands to pull them, speedily terminated its existence. First the south portions with the slated roof were brought down with a crash, then, on Midsummer Day, the well-built ancient west gable, with its great window, the limit of the church in that direction, was overthrown.*

Beautifully carved stones and tracery were discovered in the ruins and in the earthen floor, at a depth of two and a half feet, numerous skeletons continue to be laid bare. Some were accompanied by the remains of coffins, nails etc. The human relics were collected and laid to rest under the vicar's directions in the cemetery at Berry Tower.

The fact should be of no surprise that skeletons were unearthed in 1969 and again with the recent new granite paving across Mount Folly. On leaving Mount Folly steps you are walking through the former Friary cemetery and church. This, together with advice from the Cornwall Archaeological Unit, County Hall, Truro, that Mount Folly is today around three feet lower, indicates why human remains come so readily to light.

Crockwell Street

Bodmin's Crockwell Street is being regenerated after a number of years' decline. It will bring life back into what was a key part of the town centre.

In the 1831 Bodmin Register, the street was called Prison Lane after the Debtors' Prison which occupied the *'Hole in the Wall Inn'* site until 1779. Prior to the Bodmin Water Act 1866, Crockwell Street had its own well and pump to serve local houses, perhaps the name crock i.e., earthenware pot or jar, coupled with a well gives us a possible indication of name source.

A Mrs R Crockwell was ladies' secretary to the Royal Cornwall Golf Club on the outskirts of Bodmin in January 1930 - another little twist to the street name.

The main occupations of Crockwell Street residents in 1881 were:

Alfred Wendon - fitter at Goal Lane gas works; Edward Jas Levers - Cornish Arms; Martha Hore - grocer; Elizabeth Annie Seccombe - Milliner; William Standlick - grocer; John Coleman - cordwainer (shoemaker or worker in leather); William Henwood - tailor; John Nicholls Henderson - mason; Alfred Rawlings - wheelwright; William Henry Jago - butcher; Jane Edward - baker.

The town leat over the years was a constant cause of concern with severe flooding at times; during the great storm of 1936 the water was waist high. Great damage was experienced within the cottages, and stock within shops written off. The local reporter said bottles and barrels of beer were floating in the Cornish Arms. However, the police advised that no one had reported to them any floating outside the Cornish Arms.

The leat now, of course, has been refurbished and we are advised that we should be able to withstand the worst in the next 100 years. While the work was being carried out it was interesting to see how the town grew by observing the materials used. From the Priory area, granite was used a great deal. By the time the town expanded to Crockwell Street massive slabs of slate were being used to cover the leat and build over the top.

Crockwell Street was very much a place of cottages, shops, pubs and various businesses. It was also the home of the original fire station. The hand-drawn fire cart that was manned by volunteers can be seen in the Town Museum.

One well-known Bodmin figure was James Hugo who had a dyeing and cleaning business. This trade was carried on, together with his sons, for almost one hundred years on Crockwell Street. However, one son Bob ran a business in external painting and was the specialist in Cornwall for high quality work particularly when painting was to be grained, or of the marble variety. His best work was always done with his finger or thumb; so cleverly was it accomplished that it was impossible without touching the framework to differentiate between the imitation and the original. Okes, artists and photographers, was another well known business of that time.

The cinema which opened in 1921 caused great excitement on April 1930 with the first of the talkies to be shown called 'Broadway Melody' followed the next week by a film starring Al Jolson.

The 1831 Register records the following inns: Cornish Arms, Union Inn, and Colly's Beer House.

The Bodmin licensing sessions met March 13th 1914 to discuss the licence of 'The Board' Crockwell Street, during which Deputy Chief Constable Banfield stated there were a total of 14 licences in the borough, there being 339 inhabitants to each licence.

The only objector pointed out the premises were situated at the bottom of a yard, with no accommodation whatever for man other than for drinking purposes, and no accommodation for horses and traps. In close proximity were The White Hart Hotel and Cornish Arms Hotel, fully licensed, having all-round facilities.

However these objections were not sustained. The licensee, Mr J C Jayne, stated he had held a six day licence since 1908, becoming tenant under a 21 year lease. The licence was a very old one as the business had been carried on by the family for over 40 years.

Mr Buscombe outside flooded shop (1903)

Mr Jayne's death was recorded in December 1940. The family association goes back to 1874 with the wine and spirit store known as 'The Board'. It is interesting to note that Mr Jayne was a strict tee-totaller and non-smoker. What was 'The Board' we know, today, as the *'Hole in the Wall Inn'*.

Looking Forward – Berry Tower

It is generally thought that the oldest part of the town of Bodmin is close to the parish church where St Guron established his cell but, equally, the Berry area of the old cemetery including Berry Tower could be said to be just as ancient. The early 14th century Gotha Manuscript held in the British Museum and dealing with the lives of saints, suggests that the settlement on the hill was at the Berry, because a place such as this, having a cemetery. stone cross and Holy Well in close proximity to each other, probably has a Celtic origin.

Tradition, indeed persistent tradition down through the centuries, has been that Bodmin centred upon this northern hill and the fact that three Guilds were established here, points to a community of some size having been formed. In the 1530s the Prior granted a licence to hold a fair or market at this spot.

A letter from the Cornwall Archaeological Unit dated April 1993 makes interesting reading: the history of the site is very ancient and important. It seems that this area was the site of the monastery of Dinuurin, seat of the Cornish bishops in the 9th century AD, having originally been dedicated to St Guron and later replaced by St Petroc. This was a companion foundation to the other very early monastic site at Bodmin Church founded in the 6th century AD.

Berry Tower from Mount Folly

By 1470 there were three Guild chapels on the hill, thus continuing the Christian tradition. The Chapel of the Holy Rood was the largest with its chapel and burial ground. The presence of a burial ground at a Guild chapel is rare and reflects on the early monastic origins of the site. Today only the tower remains but in the 19th century foundation walls of the Chapel of the Holy Rood were traceable.

The Guild would have been a secular or religious group (perhaps like a Rotary Club or the Chamber of Commerce today) that would have paid a priest to say masses on their behalf. Between 1501 and 1514 the tower was added to the chapel. By extraordinary good fortune the

21

detailed and complete building records of the tower survive in the Cornwall Record Office. This is most unusual and adds considerably to the significance of the Tower.

Berry Tower was built on a seasonal basis between Easter and Harvest. The larger pieces of stone came from Bodiniel quarry in the vicinity of Bodmin Gaol, whereas the fine worked granite for window/door arches came from the St Austell area. The battlements and pinnacles that once adorned the top of the tower would have been shaped from Bodmin Moor granite.

A wood and iron crane transported from St Issey was used, hauling stone up internally as the tower progressed. The tower stands 50 feet tall and the crane would have had to be raised at each level. One master mason stayed with the project throughout and other tradesmen called upon when necessary.

In the British Museum one of three Bodmin churches depicted on a 16th century chart appears from its elevated situation to be that at the Berry and is shown apparently in a state of completion.

From the *Royal Cornwall Gazette* dated 8th March 1806: "Died last week at Egloshayle a venerable old lady of 112 years who is reported to have been christened in the old Berry Tower which stands north of Bodmin." If the chapel possessed a font and baptismal rights in the 1690s it must have been recognised as a Chapel of Ease.

The graveyard was used for grazing until it was purchased in 1859 for use as the town's cemetery.

A new chapter in the life of Berry Tower sees Darrock and Brown, the competitive tender winners for the project work, scaffolding the entire tower structure which is the first phase of the 16-week project to stabilise and restore the early 16th century Berry Tower.

Bodmin Town Council are extremely pleased to see Darrock & Brown, a local firm, Bodmin-based, win the contract for this restoration project and look forward to working with them over the next few months. Given their considerable expertise in this type of work, David Scott of Scott & Co, Chartered Surveyors and Historic Building Consultants (Truro) were employed as the Council's agents to co-ordinate this programme of work.

The project on completion will see the construction of a new spiral staircase leading to a viewing platform which will give the people and visitors to Bodmin a unique view of the town and its surrounding area. Once this work has been completed public access to the viewing platform will be permitted through prior arrangement with Bodmin Town Council. All of this work is being undertaken with the highest levels of sensitivity given the Tower's location within the old cemetery which also has conservation area status. Darrock and Brown have experience in working in this environment, given their previous conservation work involving Truro and Plymouth cathedrals and various churches throughout the county.

The total cost of the project is £120,000 with funds coming from the Heritage Lottery Fund (£90,000), County Environmental Trust Ltd (CET) (£12,000), the remaining balance provided by Bodmin Town Council and North Cornwall District Council.

After the construction phase of the project it is intended to undertake geophysics/ground probing radar survey work to assess the archaeology in the area. This information will be incorporated into the interpretation/information boards included on site as part of the project work. The project proved to be very successful and was completed in 2004.

Berry Tower remains a reminder of our ancient and historic past, a testimony of the skills of our forefathers, five centuries of constant watch over the town.

© PD

H M Prison, Bodmin (ca. 1900)

BTM

Bodmin Gaol - you can huff, you can puff, but you cannot blow the walls down

Bodmin has a number of imposing Victorian buildings from a period in the town's history when Cornwall was administered from the centre of Cornwall.

Bodmin Gaol, or to use the more accepted spelling Bodmin Jail, is solidly built of local stone, quarried in the immediate vicinity, giving a warmer feel and appearance to what could have been a cold, oppressive and austere looking building. The gatehouse, in particular, shows an architect willing to use the stone to his advantage by giving the impression of entering a French chateau or castle keep, an image perhaps lost on the poor unfortunates arriving to serve their sentence. The quality of workmanship was most apparent when the jail was sold in 1929. Although the slate and roof timbers etc were taken, the stone walls withstood the explosions of dynamite and still stand today as a tribute to the architect and the workmen.

Away from the hangings that have captured the public's imagination over the years, Bodmin Jail was an enlightened institution and the prisoners, male and female, were given employment and fed and clothed in a manner appropriate to the day. The sentences could be harsh but that was the role of the judiciary; the prison's role was to ensure the convicted completed the sentence given. Limited education was available and health issues addressed for male and female alike, to try and lift their prospects on release.

For some unfortunates though you could not help but think out of sight, out of mind. They were the very underdogs of society, the illiterate and physically disabled, at a time of great poverty. They would be arrested for begging, placed in jail and on completion of their sentence discharged with nothing, having to beg again and be re-arrested. A life cycle that does not bear thinking about today.

The civil prison closed in 1916 and the section operated by the Admiralty as a Navy Prison ceased in 1922. In 1927 the whole jail was formerly closed and all the buildings sold in 1929.

Dudley Prout Collection

Bodmin Riding

©WHJ

Keeping a tradition alive

Cornwall throughout the centuries, has celebrated its customs including the 'Obby 'Oss at Padstow, the Furry Dance at Helston, and Hurling the Silver Ball through St Columb. Bodmin has 'the Riding' that takes place on or near to July 7th, St Thomas Beckett Day, an indication perhaps of a medieval origin, as the Thomas Beckett Chantry to the east of St Petroc's Church was completed in the 14th century. Incidentally, the Chantry within the Church grounds is well worthy of a visit to see, in particular the east facing window which has outstanding tracery and is a rare example within Cornwall.

James Ferguson Lith.

VIEW OF BODMIN CHURCH AND ST. THOMAS'S CHAPEL FROM THE EAST.

The Riding, as implied, was a procession on horseback paraded in and around the town, together with a band playing the Riding Air. Tradition ensured a special brew of Riding Ale accompanied the Riders and the Town Crier, whose cry would be to householders 'to the people of this house, a prosperous morning, long life, health and a merry riding.' The householder then tasted the ale and made a contribution to expenses. It is thought the Town Guilds kept the tradition, receiving garlands in Priory Park and carrying emblems of their crafts, before proceeding to Church, followed by two days of celebration and sports.

The ceremony lapsed in early Victorian times as celebrations, together with perhaps too much ale tasting, did not find favour with the impact of Methodism and Non-Conformist teetotalism of that particular period.

However, eventually a revival took place and today the lively Riding Air can be heard through the town as the garlanded horses and riders process keeping a tradition alive as a reminder of our rich and ancient history.

©*WHJ*

The Robes of Death
Fine clothes may have brought us the plague

One day there came into Bodmin strange carriers with a long string of pack-mules laden with goods, the like of which had never been seen in Cornwall before. There were rich robes and plumed hats, velvet gowns and silk dresses, ribbons of bright hues, gloves and laces, such as were worn by the Court ladies.

These goods were sold by the packmen at such remarkably low prices that the stock was rapidly exhausted. The vendors then promptly left, with no time to obtain victuals, no time to exchange gossip. They and their pack mules disappeared leaving behind a grim legacy masked as benevolence.

"Black Death" the plague that knew no friends, had arrived in Bodmin together with the terrible knowledge that the fine clothes townspeople had been so eager to buy were infected with the pestilence which had devastated London. The garments were quickly collected and burnt, but it was too late to stay the course of the disease.

The Black Death visited Bodmin to devastate the town from a period 1348 to around 1350 during which time some 1500 people died.

Could it have arrived in infected clothing? Well, the answer must be "yes" but perhaps we should look to the records of the clergy for another indication with more substance. The clergy must have fallen wholesale, and as each fell another was ready at his Bishop's call fearlessly to fill the vacant place. Apparently the plague was carried by sea and penetrated inland. In the March we learn of a new incumbent at Fowey, a week later one at St Winnow, higher up the River Fowey, and on the 22nd March the sickness at Bodmin. Two brothers of the Priory wrote to the Bishop that all and every one of their brethren had died, therefore they could not elect a new prior.

"Black Death" the plague which swept across Europe in the years 1348-1350 beginning in the ports of Italy - it was the worst scourge ever known to man; at least a quarter of the European population was wiped out in the first epidemic of 1348.

It was transmitted to humans by fleas from black rats, though this was not known at the time. The epidemic which raged in England in 1665 wiped out whole villages and one tenth of London's population of 460,000. Samuel Pepys wrote a grim account of it in his diary.

It appeared to have entered England near Weymouth circa August 1348. It lingered longer in Cornwall and Devon than elsewhere, perhaps due to a scattered rural population. Records show that the output of tin fell to an all-time low and moorland animals with no one to look after them died in their hundreds.

In the strange way of fate though, the Black Death caused much progress to be made from the medieval to the modern and helped the abolition of serfdom on account of the scarcity of labour it created. The power of the lords, among them those of the church, was temporarily weakened as the remaining labourers were naturally in demand and could afford to assert themselves. By May of 1350 the Duke of Cornwall, in view of the great distress authorised his agents to remit one-fourth part of the rent of the tenants who were left, for fear they should, through poverty, depart from holdings. So, perhaps, even in the worst of all devastation there has to be a glimmer of hope.

From the engraving *'Dr Beak of Rome'* by Paul Furst (Rome 1656). This plague doctor is wearing the following protective clothing: hat, long waxed cloak, a mask containing herbs and spices, believed to prevent the plague, crystal eye protection and a rod to help in the examination of the patients, without touching them.

Pigs, corsets and the curate of Bodmin

How many pig dealers lived in Bodmin in the mid 19th century? Who were the business people? What trades were carried on? The 1851 census of Bodmin reveals a great deal.

A number of mining families had arrived to work in local copper, tin and lead mines and it is most interesting to look at the children's places of birth to see how they followed the work from West Cornwall. Traditionally, some of the wives and daughters worked as ore dressers (bal maidens) hard manual work at the surface, while their husbands and sons, perhaps as young as fourteen, learned their trade underground.

Although in one agricultural labourer's family in Nanstallon village, John was recorded as a miner and working in local mines at the age of nine. This was an extreme case, but it was not unusual for a child of eleven to start work as a farm labourer or servant. It is very interesting to see four mining families living at Blowing House, for the words 'Blowing House' refer to the act of tin smelting and it is thought tin streaming occurred in the locality.

Honey Street was a marvellous mix of people and trades typical of a West Country market town - a veterinary surgeon, barrister, carver and guilder, surgeon, watchmaker, shoemaker, Chelsea Pensioner, cooper, nurse, inn keeper, grocer, stone mason, saddler, postmaster, tallow chandler and a china dealer.

But, of course, for some the onset of old age and an agricultural tied cottage could mean only one thing - the Union Workhouse. Here, with other unfortunates, they eked out a miserable existence, A short story by Quiller-Couch puts into words the tragedy and emotions suffered by those destined by fate to the Workhouse.

We also had in our midst the County Gaol (Jail) where the Governor was from Sheerness and a number of wardens from Devonport, no doubt all with some experience of the dreaded prison hulks moored in the Tamar. As for the inmates, they were listed by age from 12 year old Charles from Falmouth, of no occupation, to a 72 year old seaman from Ireland. The females were of a similar age grouping with a Mary-Ann keeping her 5 year old son with her.

At the Cornwall Lunatic Asylum there were 110 male and 113 female occupants.

Leaving those institutions, which perhaps presented a darker side of Bodmin we go to the vibrant, bustling market town that Bodmin was. At

31

Oliver's Hotel, later The Royal Hotel, in Fore Street, in addition to the innkeeper and his family, resided a private governess, a bar maid, tap maid, 3 chambermaids, under bar maid, 2 cooks, kitchen maid, 2 house maids, ostler, under ostler and a waiter. A document exhibited at the hotel stated that in 1847, the proprietor, William Oliver, was appointed postmaster to the establishment of Her Majesty's stables in Bodmin. In the latter part of the 19th century Mr Augustus Coombe Sandoe was the proprietor, at one time keeping as many as 60 horses for posting purposes.

Fore Street, like Honey Street, catered for virtually any merchandise you could wish to purchase, from hats to shoes, from saddles to medicine, with professions as diverse as an artist on glass to a corset maker, with an auctioneer and the curate of Bodmin for good measure.

The Cornwall 1851 census 'Parish of Bodmin' is an interesting social document of our history. It will also provide the answer as to how many pig dealers actually did live in the parish.

© Kathy Keen

Escaping the census! A delightful photograph taken when two pigs were out for a summer evening stroll in North Cornwall.

A Dickensian Christmas
in Bodmin - the historic county town of Cornwall

Approaching Christmas it is a far cry from the year of 1854 and through the writings of John Burton in 1904 we can capture the hustle and bustle, the very atmosphere of a market town as he puts it "in full swing".

In those days there were tanners, hatters, glovers and basket workers. Mines were working in close proximity to the town, Boscarne, Wheal Keckwich, Wheal Messer, Trebell and Prince of Wales - all in the parish of Lanivet. The Royal Cornwall Rangers Militia, a thousand strong, was located and billeted in the town all through the Crimean War, 1854-55. The men were dressed in bottle green suits with swallow-tail coats. Hundreds of navvies were cutting the Cornwall Railway who obtained their provisions etc at Bodmin Market, and a rough lot they were. There was no safety for fowls, pigs, geese and ducks. If they only heard a cock crowing on a Saturday night, they would certainly steal it for Sunday's dinner. There were no police in those days, only parish constables. One notorious navvy, by the name of 'Nipper Jack' would often be seen in the stocks outside the Market House for getting drunk and refusing to pay the fine. He would be smoking his pipe with all the bravado imaginable and chaffer everyone passing by.

The streets were simply lined with covered and uncovered stalls, with merchandise extending from Oliver's Royal Hotel on one side of Fore Street and from the Guildhall on the other side, to and including Mount Folly. Passengers on the old mail coaches had been heard to remark that Bodmin, on market days, resembled a continental fair with its quaint and varied stalls.

In the Market House the stalls were occupied by a number of butchers from Bodmin, Lostwithiel and the surrounding villages. Geese were in abundance on the stalls at this time.

Leaving the Market House, coming down the street to the left were lollipop stalls, Rundall's rope stall, Maunder's (Lostwithiel) wood turnery stall with bowls, chairs etc, Hendy - hatter, Cullis - glover, Stephens - glover and Bazeley - hatter. Nearer the Town Clock, London Inn and the Fountain Inn were George Passmore's cake and liquor stall selling hot pies etc, Chapman's sweetmeats, John Wilmot's fancy stall and Joe Skellet's swag stall.

Crossing over the street on a busy Christmas time market day, with the horse traffic, also perhaps a wet day, the shoppers would have had to contend with mud and puddles, causing the women and girls to lift their dresses well above the ankles and step with care.

Going back up Fore Street from the foot of Mount Folly steps stood the lollipop and orange stalls which extended up as far as the Guildhall. The stallholders were lively characters for example, Joicy Hawke, who really was a good saleswoman and would talk and blink enough to stop a clock working and Cally May, a very stout, good tempered old soul, who was very celebrated for her California rock, which gave every boy in Bodmin toothache. Plant and vegetable stalls, book stalls, and cutlery stalls also lined the street. There was Jack Brown, a Cockney razor paste man, with a waiter tray in front of him, with his stock in trade, chopping sticks with his razor to show the quality of his paste and Jimmy Williams, a tall cross-eyed man, with his waiter tray, selling ointment for the cure of warts, corns and bunions, to whom John Burton gave testimonial for curing a troublesome corn he had on his shoulder, caused he said through wearing too tight a shirt.

At the foot of the Mount Folly steps stood gardener Hicks, seedman, and old Jim Saundry with his home-made tools and ironware from Bridges. Opposite was Billy Williams' jewellery stall and on top of the steps to the right through the centre of Mount Folly (North to south) ran a long range of quaint covered boot and shoe stalls.

Just above was the Corn Market House (now Public Rooms) where the farmers used to sell corn which was brought into the town on horseback, then came a range of crockery stalls and near the railings were cheap-jack vans, potato carts, and apple carts. At the further end were George Climo (Georgie Profit) and Jim Jewell with live pigs in carts.

Near the Assize hall were cows, calves and Goss Moor ponies, sold by old Sammy Gingerbread. Underneath Mount Folly was a range of fish stalls, 'Billy Peppermint' with his wheel of fortune, quack doctors and old Jack Perry (Blind Jack) and the St Day George Ballad Singers.

Here then a picture has been painted in words of how Bodmin in the 1800s would have been on a market day before Christmas. Today one would suppose that Heritage Day, with its stalls, is as near as we will get to those

days when shopping and life in general had more than its share of character. But for now, from Joicy Hawke, Georgie Profit and the rest of the cast of 1854, too many to mention, we wish One and All a very merry Christmas and a very peaceful New Year.

A day out in Bodmin in 1936

The year is 1936, the townspeople were looking forward to the hospital carnival. It ran its course under expert guidance from its chairman, Mr Norman Lyne and secretaries Mr Norman Bricknell and Mr V T Hore. The carnival queen "Her Majesty" for the day Miss Pearl Osborne and her Maids of Honour, Misses Eileen Rowe and Phyllis Stentiford, and all the bands paraded through the town with the excitement and good humour all carnivals generate.

But what of the businesses in the town 70 years ago?

Well, to travel to the carnival we could contact Willis Central Garage who has 14 and 20 seater modern coaches for hire, or R G Reed, the Bodmin & Park Garages, Austin agent with cars for hire - just pick up a phone and dial 9 for Bodmin. For the rest, Giles Wright in Fore Street, agent for Raleigh Cycles and authorised repairer for H M Post Office for over 16 years, offers every accommodation for your cycle during the carnival week. Whilst, W Goss, in Honey Street, will part-exchange the cycle you ride in on and you can return in style on a brand new Hercules or BSA model.

So now you have arrived to join the rest of us, what has Bodmin, to offer?

Of the large stores, International claims shopping is a pleasure with them. Home & Colonial for the finest groceries, the Co-op advertises best materials, clean packing and full weight, without the packing. Frisby's shoes, claim to be one of 130 branches and shopping with them is a pleasure, and remind us to look good on carnival day. Marshalls of Fore Street and Mount Folly have made-to-measure suits at thirty nine shillings and sixpence, Jaegar wear and Dak's trousers. J Brewer and Son are retailing Radiac shirts, Aquatite raincoats from 21 pennies and Hepworths in Fore Street, state "worth" does not appear in their name by accident. Kendalls of 6 Fore Street are selling wool-linked silk hose in new shades from one and sixpence halfpenny and Kiltie shoes for Five Toes.

From Lawrence's Central House you can purchase Aertex shirts, vests and trunks. A look in Zimber's jewellers window reminds you of the time before your hair appointment at Maison Louis at Mount Folly for a permanent waving at 12 shillings and sixpence, or you may be going to A Hicks, opposite the Constitutional Club, who now have extra staff and accommodation to provide a quicker service, with perms priced from 10 shillings to 21 shillings.

Afterwards you may fancy a meal or a cup of tea. There is Adrian & Dawe, Central Cafe, at 1 Bore Street, J Pascoe at Higher Bore Street (noted for their fish and chips), R Weary and the Phoenix Restaurant and Brewers (Bakers) Ltd. Town Wall Cafe claim that the same ingredients are used in making bread on the Queen Mary as they use "get the best out of life - eat Brewer's bread." Finally, the Chestnuts Cafe and Guest House, Fore Street offer free car parking to patrons.

Other businesses in existence at this time are J Phil Brown, butchers at Honey Street; George H Spear, Priors Barn Dairy offering pure new milk from healthy cows, delivered twice daily in bottles; Hellen Universal Stores, established 1871 with deliveries by motor vans up to a 15 mile radius. Thos. Vincent, in Bree Shute Lane, tells us our complexion is alright but is our car's? For less than the cost of four new tyres they will change its complexion with 40 shades to choose from. Broad, Bray & Solomon, Pool Street, motor body and wagon builders build vehicles of every description to order. At Premier Garage, Church Square you can buy a new Popular Ford saloon car for £100 plus £6 tax.

Back in the town again you can purchase films for your camera, Agfa, Kodak, Selo or Cine from Date Chemist, Honey Street or Sydney Northey, Chemists at Turret House.

A final look around the shops, 3 piece suites are on sale at Goodfellow & Sons from £7 10 shillings. Gas or electric?, a difficult choice. Bodmin Electricity Supply advise you to save money -"cooking-heating-lighting" - one penny halfpenny per unit, water heating three quarters of a penny per unit" - ring Bodmin 94 but Bodmin Gas Consumers Co Ltd claim that gas is the cheapest -"buy a new gas cooker from half a penny a week, enamelled in any colour finish, chromium plated taps, plate rack and automatic oven control - a pleasure to cook with" - ring Bodmin 95.

I hope that this shopping day in Bodmin in 1936 has brought back many happy memories. No doubt, there are many businesses that we have not had time to visit. Bodmin - in 1936, as it is today, a market town serving all of the surrounding villages and townsfolk alike.

Carnival Prize-winning Window Display at Marshall's.

36

The day Bodmin was bombed

Bodmin's only serious air raid during the 1939-45 War occurred on 7th August 1942 and killed nine people, eight of them being members of one family.

It was a Friday lunchtime when two Focke-Wulf light bombers came In low over the sea at Par to make one of the tip and run raids which the German Air Force was then making on towns and villages in the south west.

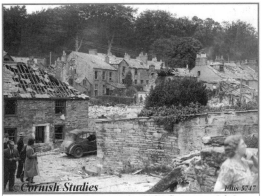

Cornish Studies   Ellis 5747

The bomb damage in Mill Street, which claimed nine lives.

The two planes swept over Par, to sight up on the River Fowey and follow it as far as Bodmin Road Station, here banking to the left. They now had a direct run to their target - the town of Bodmin.

Mr Edwin Renals of Wadebridge was cycling from Fletchers Bridge when one plane roared overhead. "The planes' markings and the pilot were quite visible," he later told the local press. Less than a minute later the planes dived low over Bodmin, dropped two five hundred pound bombs and gave continuous cannon shell fire as they flew over the town.

The first bomb was a direct hit on Primrose Dairy, Mill Street, killing 16 year old Edgar Tippett. Instead of burying into the ground, the bomb exploded on impact with a concrete machine bed, which in turn spread the blast sideways. The family reunion of the Sargent family in the house next door ended in tragedy. Mr William Sargent survived, but he lost eight members of his family representing three generations, who were all together in their cottage for a celebration. A good many other houses were badly damaged and for a time four hundred people were homeless.

To add to the problem, Bodmin was without a piped water supply, for the main had been shattered when a bomb fell at St Breward the previous day. The town was dependent on Church Stile and Cock's Well for its water.

The second bomb fell and exploded between two gas holders, one full and the other empty. The blast was lessened because the bomb buried deep into the ground before exploding. Miraculously, the full gas holder did not explode as red hot shrapnel pierced the side to let out flaming gas as it slowly sank to the ground. For the Fire Brigade quickly in attendance, it was a very worrying and extremely dangerous time.

Several staff and workmen were injured, including Miss Irene Knight, whose Gas Works office was demolished and she was buried under rubble for two hours, before being rescued.

Strange incidents often accompany this type of major incident. A bizzare incident occurred with Primrose Diary. The bombed four-storey warehouse which contained a considerable amount of butter and margarine was seen to go up in a ball of flames. The nearby houses, badly damaged by the initial explosion, then received a splattered coating of butter and margarine. Another concerned a black cat which was discovered under the rubble at the Gas Works eight days after the bombing. The cat was rescued by enticing it with a saucer of milk well-laced with brandy and it made a remarkable recovery.

As the planes climbed away, they spotted a goods train making its run to Bodmin General from Boscarne junction. They swooped down, opened fire, shelling the train. For the railway men involved, this was an even more frightening experience due to the fact that this was an ammunitions train. It was a miracle that there were no casualties.

Pool Street after the bombing

A total of 19,145 bombs of all kinds were dropped on Cornwall between 5th July 1940 and 30th May 1944 (just under 140 bombs per fatality). 102 civilians and 37 military personnel were killed, 250 seriously injured and 223 slightly injured. 20 servicemen were killed at RAF St Eval Aerodrome.

Had the bomb at the Gas Works exploded on surface impact the statistics would have been greatly increased and the effect on Bodmin would have been even more devastating.

Tomatoes - Votes - Humour, Elections Past

With a general election soon to be upon us, let us look back and in doing so try not to be too conservative in our outlook, too liberal in view or labour under any preconceptions, in fact I hope taking an independent line.

In 1974 former MP Paul Tyler entered the record book with the 12th lowest recorded majority, obtaining a nine vote win over the sitting member, Robert Hicks, who eight months later regained the Bodmin constituency.

Another record, set in Cornwall, was at Launceston in 1874. Mr H S Gifford, a Conservative, who received only one vote in a by-election, he later claimed he had been entered without his consent (but one has to wonder where the one vote came from).

In 1658 Cornwall could boast of 44 MPs and up until 1867 Bodmin had two MPs to represent the borough.

The Temperance Society in 1835 petitioned Parliament urging "for the more effectual suppression of treating drunkenness at elections", this followed the Bodmin election when the proposed MPs provided, out the goodness of their hearts, "bands, cockades, ribbons, meat and drinks in excess of £4000" so the voters went in a state of intoxication to the polls! Mind you, the Temperance Society had their hands full at that time with there being 29 public houses in Bodmin.

In 1833 Mr Samuel Spry, MP for Bodmin, generously gave £200 to be expended in the purchase of blankets and shoes, which were distributed to the poor in the borough, who produced a ticket from an elector who had voted for Mr Spry. In the same year stood the Spry Arms Inn on the south side of Town Wall and thought to be named after him.

I do like the story from Lostwithiel. Around election time a freeholder came into the town mounted on a donkey, he in the colours of Pendarves and his donkey in the colours of Vyvyan. When this was queried he stated he and his ass had been long standing friends and would never come to blows over politics, so they decided to wear the colours of who they would vote for. In other words, only an ass would vote for V...

The most famous figure to stand and be elected for Bodmin, was without doubt Isaac Foot. A staunch Methodist, he liked nothing better than to conduct his meetings with all the excitement and fervour of a Methodist revival meeting. Isaac relished hecklers and there were many at his meetings to keep the pot boiling. He held the seat in 1923, was defeated in 1924 and returned again in 1929. Surely it was here that a young Michael Foot served his apprenticeship as an orator and politician. With hecklers, Isaac was never lost for words. Women in 1910 would call out to him "Vote for Pole-Carew". Back would shout Isaac "Cock-doodle-do." "Are you Jewish, Isaac?" and he would riposte "No, but I intend to be one of the chosen few." Further calls and questions would rain fast and furious, to one Isaac replied "My dear man, I can give you the answers to your questions, but I cannot give you the brains to understand." Rotten tomatoes would be thrown, but perhaps a full hour of vociferous speech, rollicking humour and invective, fifteen minutes of passionate argument and a peroration to take the roof off the Old Market in Fore Street.

What political times to have lived in.

© *Cornish Studies*

Bodmin Candidates, their Wives and Agents (June 1945)
L to R: Cdr. Marshall *(Conservative)*, Mrs. Marshall, Mr. J H Pitts *(Labour)*, Mrs. Pitts, Mr. Ford *(Liberal Agent)*, Mrs. Foot, Maj. J Foot *(Liberal)*, Mr. A H Hitchens *(Labour Agent)* and Mr. Newton Clare *(Conservative Agent)*.

For whom the Ball tolled

The Toll House at Priors Barn (October 1933)

This photograph of the toll house on the Plymouth Road reminds me of an incident that took place in February 1950 when the Ball family lived there. Little Vera Ball who was looking forward to her Birthday party, was gazing out of the window when there was a vivid blue flash. The window was thrown out and she was thrown to the floor, lightening had struck the house with such severity that the ceiling collapsed on top of her. A passing lorry driver found Mrs Ball and Vera in a dazed and shocked state, for the roof was almost completely demolished, every ceiling had come down and one wall was badly damaged with windows torn from the frames.

However, all was not lost for Vera, as when the furniture was removed that day, the fancy cakes and jellies were found to be intact and the party was held in her auntie's house in Green Lane, the following day.

The lightening also caused the electricity supply in the town to be off completely for half an hour.

Another great storm had hit the town forty-seven years before in 1903, flooding Church Square to a depth of three feet and sweeping away the bridge at Laveddon; it was one of the most disastrous floods in the memory of any living person. Rain had fallen perpetually for some weeks with an abnormal fall on the Tuesday morning resulting in many bridges being washed away and numerous buildings being destroyed.

Bodmin LSWR Station (later Bodmin North) was under water and the Fire Brigade were kept busy at The Bodmin Gas Works, Berrycombe Road, pumping out water to avoid a possible explosion. Church Square, Honey Street and Crockwell Street suffered badly owing to the town leat being unable to cope, and with the filthy water two or three feet deep, stocks in most shops were ruined and householders in despair. St Breward was badly affected with the De Lank Quarries flooded and closing down.

At Dunmere the situation was desperate, large trees were floating in the River Camel, and at Dunmere Mill, the residence of Mr and Mrs J Hawke, Mrs Hawke tried to finish dinner with the water rising all around her, until finally the chickens were washed out of the oven and lost! She then urged her sons to find dry wood, and lighting a fire in the bedroom made tea for the helpers, a woman of great fortitude, I think. The fowl in the fowl house were swept away downstream at great speed and lost, but the pigs swam for it and managed to get ashore in the woods owned by Mr Lobb, just down the valley.

Mention must be made of the mineral train driver's heroic efforts when Wenford Bridge collapsed. He raced his train, with the whistle blowing furiously, down that twisty track to warn farmers who had not already moved their stock from river fields, leaning from his cab and shouting the news at the top of his voice all the way.

Further down stream at Boscarne, the newly opened wooden bridge stood the weight of the water until the afternoon when it dislodged, and floated like Noah's Ark on the flood in the direction of Nanstallon, the promised land perhaps.

The bridge at Laveddon was swept away, traffic being sent via Treluggon Moor or St Lawrence's, but when the floods subsided, railway sleepers were brought from Bodmin for a temporary bridge to enable traffic to reach Lanivet.

Hard to believe when we enjoyed a welcome rest at Blowinghouse on this year's Beating of the Bounds (1989) that the stream we were to follow through Laveddon and St Lawrence's to the River Camel could become a dangerous raging torrent sweeping all before it.

Mr W L Twinning from Bodmin had the unusual experience when returning from Wadebridge on a shopping trip of finding himself afloat on his horse and trap at Sladesbridge, he said his horse had to swim through the flood and only with God's guiding hand they reached dry land and safety.

On the east side of Bodmin two bridges were lost on a tributary to the River Fowey near Glynn House, and Lostwithiel was badly flooded with boats conveying passengers to and from the railway station.

If we step back further in history to July 16th 1847, a waterspout burst on Davidstow Moor and roared down the River Camel with a wall of water said to be twelve to eighteen feet high. For many years afterwards, people in the valleys could point to debris lodged twenty feet up in the trees as a reminder of the great flood. All bridges, with the exception of Helland and Wadebridge, were destroyed, a truly terrifying spectacle for all who witnessed it.

Wartime: pomp and ceremony, fun and some sadness

Much has been written of how Cornwall survived the war years but let us look through the local paper and see how Bodmin fared, one month in 1944, in those difficult times. The paper presented a fine balance of war-time Cornwall and life having to go on in very much the same old way, if at all possible.

Justice Lawrence reflected this in his arrival at the parish church for a service and subsequent conveyance to the Assize Hall for the opening of the court in a carriage drawn by two prancing bay horses. High Sheriff, Mr Michael P Williams, who provided the carriage, said, "I take no interest in motor cars whatever, but I am fond of horses and I think they look the part". The local reporter, however, faced castigation from one reader the following week, who stated, "the horses were as definitely a pair of chestnuts as I ever saw in my life".

For Judge Lawrence, though, it was a busy first day dealing with nine criminal cases of which four dealt with under age sex, one incest case and one bigamy, perhaps it was no wonder he was in need of a church service to start his day.

©Cornwall Studies Ellis 48074

Mr Justice Berry leaving the Shire House to walk to the Assize Court. He carries a posy of herbs to combat the smells of prisoners and others attending the Assizes.

American army stores found in the possession of a local woman was the subject of charges brought in court. A Mrs H.... pleaded not guilty, stating that 23 cakes of soap were given to her son by a white American soldier. A blanket left on her garden wall was given by a black American soldier, one mackintosh coat was given to her son by a black American soldier and one steel helmet was given to her son who exchanged it for a penknife. Mrs H...., when questioned, said she thought the American soldiers had a right to give things away. The judge, who did not share her generous opinion, imposed a hefty £8 fine.

Special Services for men taking part in the invasion of Northern France were held in the Parish Church, Lady Huntingdon's Church and Town Wall Church on the Tuesday evening.

A photograph caption stated that a blackcap had nested in the post box at Hengar, near St. Tudy and had laid seven eggs; mother and eggs were doing well.

Bodmin Borough Council reported that the Mayor had sent a telegram to Italy stating: *"On behalf of the citizens of the County Town of Cornwall, I offer sincere congratulations to the Duke of Cornwall's Light Infantry for the outstanding part that they have taken in recent successes in Italy."*

It was also agreed that a letter of sympathy be sent to Lady Arthur Quiller-Couch on the death of Sir Arthur, a native of the town.

An official notice with regard to rubber tyres informed farmers that unnecessary damage to tyres meant 90% were worn down to the canvas and was a great waste as they could not be re-treaded. If this continued it could mean farmers with rubber shod tractors having to revert to irons.

Under the lost and found column: **'Lost wheel from Morris 8 car between St Kew, Amble and Wadebridge. Reward.'** The mind boggles. Did they drive from St. Kew on three wheels? I mean was the ale that good?

Bodmin Penny-a-week Red Cross Fund for May amounted to £30-19s-7d and St. John Ambulance Brigade continued its training nights.

With the fine weather, the horse races at Coldharbour, organised by the Race Committee of the Bodmin Prisoners of War Fund, were said to be assured of success. The most popular event was rodeo riding on the lively moorland ponies.

Fire Brigade roused the town - Hengar Mansion in flames

The year 1901 saw Bodmin Fire Brigade raise sufficient funds to purchase a new horse-drawn engine which was presented to the Mayor by Captain Bawden on behalf of the brigade and was named *"Ethel"* after Captain Bawden's wife. The engine was to give valuable service for nearly thirty years.

"Ethel", Bodmin's horse drawn fire engine

November 1904 was to see *"Ethel"* attend a fire of great personal tragedy to the Onslow family. The following extract from a local paper of the day gives a sad reading:

"About ten minutes to seven on Saturday last November 11th, residents of Bodmin were aroused by the sounding of the fire bugle calling members of the brigade together. The town was soon astir, inhabitants rushing into the streets to know the scene of the fire. A few minutes previous to the call, a rider had hurried into the town from Hengar House, St Tudy, with the startling intelligence that the house was in flames and that it was in great danger of being totally destroyed before the brigade would be able to render any assistance. When the brigade arrived at the house just before eight o'clock the hopelessness of their mission was only too apparent.

The members of the family who were at Hengar House at the time of the fire included Sir William and Lady Onslow, Lieutenant Roger Onslow and three daughters. The only visitor to the house was Miss Mildred Wilmot, lady friend of the young heir. So strong was the hold the fire had obtained when discovered, that all rushed to the Long Room, a spot furthest from the seat of the fire in their night attire and there waited in the cold till some covering in the form of sheets, blankets and curtains could be procured.

Bodmin Fire Brigade, under Captain Bawden and Lieutenants Shelley and Hender, worked with their manual engine from eight in the morning till after five in the afternoon, by which time Hengar was but bare walls enclosing a blackened heap of debris. For centuries Hengar had graced the manor of St Tudy, amid its beautiful surroundings, its ivy-clad walls, giving it that venerable aspect so dear to the hearts of Englishmen. Like most other mansions it had been added to and embellished by successive owners.

The house, some portions of which were three stories high, consisted of about fifty rooms and in the principal of these, many valuable paintings, including some by Van Dyke, were hung on the walls. The portrait gallery contained the history, in portrait, of the Onslow family. Principal among the portraits was one of Admiral Sir Richard Onslow, whose Camperdown exploits brought the title to the family. Another portrait, of much value, was that of Sir Richard Onslow, M.P. for Guildford, who sided with Cromwell. Seventeen members of the Onslow family have sat for Guildford and never was an Onslow beaten for that constituency except once - by an Onslow! Only three portraits were saved. None of the family silver or jewels were saved and most of the old English furniture and china perished in the flames, but in the destruction of the paintings, perhaps, lay the greatest loss."

With many men away, the brigade carried on as well as it could in World War I. All members, not in the armed forces, became special constables. It is noted that in 1918 special drill was carried out at Bodmin Gaol, where valuable national treasures were stored, to acquaint them with the special procedures needed.

But the end of the war brought changes, and an end to an era was perhaps signalled by a rick fire in 1919 at Mr Coad's farm, Tredinnick. All of the members turned out, but there was difficulty in obtaining horses. Some were eventually procured, but when the brigade reached the farm they found that there was no suitable water supply, so they came away without doing anything. Three years later, the brigade turned for the first time to a lorry instead of horses. On receiving the alarm to a serious fire at St Breward, a lorry towed *"Ethel"*, which took one hour for the journey, and was successful in saving two of the six cottages owned by English China Clay. But in 1925 the brigade's luck ran out. Having received a call at 11.30 am, the next frustrating one and a half hours were spent trying to find a lorry to tow the engine. Eventually a lorry which was delivering in Fore Street, was able to undertake the mission.

This whole episode was the subject of letters to the press, extract as follows:

"The messenger rode into Bodmin at 11.20 am and at 12.30 pm the brigade was still going round Church square hauled by a delivery lorry from St Austell. What a scream! The matter of old 'Ethel' needs looking into. She has done good service but is now fit to make annual carnival a trifle more antiquated." Harsh words of criticism for the loyal brigade. The secretary replied stating the lorry was the first to appear in the street at that time and kindly conveyed the appliance to Bowden, Helland, and the correspondent should note that the appliances are paid for out of the Borough rates and are only intended for use inside the Borough, and outside that as one helping a neighbour in distress.

1926 saw the arrival of a motor trailer pump, paid for by public subscription and handed over to the grateful Town Council, whose Mayor, Mr A Browning-Lyne, was quick to praise the brigade and the ratepayers in general. In reply to Mr Shelley, the Chief Officer of the brigade, who stated that they wanted more money to buy a lorry to take the brigade and equipment outside the town, he said he felt there was plenty of opportunity yet for our country friends to subscribe to the fund. After all. *'Ethel'* could carry on in the town with good water pressure in the mains for some time ahead. A demonstration then took place on Mount Folly with the pump sending jets of water high over the Public rooms.

The following year saw Mr Shelley resign at the age of sixty six after fifty-one years service to the brigade, having joined at the age of fifteen, a record hard to equal in loyalty to his town, in any branch of service.

Thursday, May 10th 1928, heralded the arrival of a motor tender at a cost of £415. With its four speed gear box it was capable of 45 miles per hour and was said to be well sprung and to be as comfortable as if riding in a car. On the Friday evening, the tender towed the pump to Lanivet, where a demonstration of its powers was given to a large crowd of sightseers. The pump threw a stream of water over the church tower.

The brigade had entered a new era, that of the motor vehicle. For the motor tender, the first call outside the town, was from Mr Wills, Merryfield Farm at Temple, Bodmin Moor, in September 1928. Receiving the call at 5.55 am the brigade covered the six and a half miles and was on the scene by 6.25 am. The fire was under control by 8 o'clock with half of the hay rick and two ricks of nearby corn saved, thus proving that the expenditure for the motor tender was a very good investment indeed.

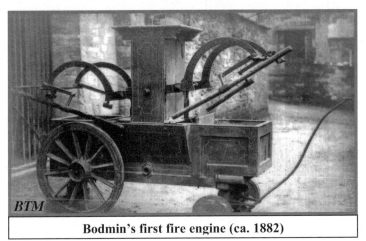

Bodmin's first fire engine (ca. 1882)

DCLI Museum

Lucknow July 1ˢᵗ – November 17ᵗʰ 1857

The Lucknow Road

India was in turmoil, the British Government had introduced an improved musket, the Enfield rifle, nothing wrong in that one would have thought, but not so.

At this time, Britain was heavily engaged in the Crimean War, leading to a severe reduction in regiments serving in India and resources were stretched to a minimum, now into this comes the Nan Sahib (who was one of the adopted sons of the last Peshwa of Bithur), living in exile at Cawnpore, a "large chip on his shoulder", a great many followers and a belief the British were very weak at that moment and the time was right for revolt. He was right and in time honoured tradition we played straight into his hands. We introduced the rifle and greased cartridges to the Bengal Army. The Hindu thought the new ammunition was greased with the fat of cows, which they considered sacred, and the Mohammedan was convinced that it was greased with the lard of swine, which was considered unclean. Inevitably rebellion occurred and on 6th May 1857 some of the Indian regiments refused to handle the cartridges, were court martialled and sentenced to hard labour as they had lit the fuse of mutiny. The following day (Sunday) congregations were butchered in churches, fugitives were killed in flight and by the end of June, British power was reduced to a few hard-pressed garrisons.

The 32nd Cornwall Foot Regiment defended Lucknow, the only town left in the province of Oudh in British hands, but the greater part of the married families of the Regiment were with a small detachment of the 32nd at Cawnpore. This little band withstood the onslaught of Nan Sahib's hordes but by the end of June their rations were exhausted, supplies had run out, so with great trepidation they accepted the Nan Sahib's offer of safe conduct to boats and freedom. In accordance with the offer the brave little garrison, the women and children, men of the 32nd with them, bayonets fixed and Captain Moore at the head, marched down to the river. There they were massacred. The 32nd Regiment lost 3 Officers, 82 other ranks, 47 women and 55 children; their bodies being thrown into deep wells.

The siege of Lucknow began earlier than expected and before defences had been completed, so it was decided to blow up a fort on the outskirts of the defence and concentrate on the defence of the residency and immediate surroundings. A Private involved in placing explosives, celebrated too early and fell asleep, only to be blown up with the fort. Falling to the ground he continued his sleep, waking up the next day to find the fort a ruin and his comrades gone. To the great surprise and merriment of the Regiment he arrived at the Residency on an ammunition cart drawn by two bullocks, the rebels too intent on their looting to notice his arrival.

The siege dragged on through July, the rebels devoting themselves to the digging of mines to undermine the garrison defences. They were foiled, however, by Cornish miners in the Regiment. July was a bad month with 170 being killed and wounded.

The garrison suffered severely from lack of medical supplies and doctors. An amputation meant death, in nearly every case. The defenders were wearied under the strain of the siege; even the physical exertion of loading and resisting the recoil of the rifles was beginning to have an effect. Several of the ladies and many of the children had succumbed, under the rebels' incessant bombardment, or by disease, for cholera, smallpox and scurvy were taking their toll.

But when the defenders of Lucknow were enduring the torments of the summer sun, wounds, disease and scarcity of food, efforts were being made to relieve their desperate plight.

Sir Henry Havelock, at the head of a Force, had reached Cawnpore and while at this place, many of his soldiers visited the wells into which the murdered had been thrown. They realised what had happened and when they left, practically every man took away with him a lock of hair, a broken toy or piece of woman's clothing. These ghastly relics of a brutal crime, they pinned inside their tunics and they did not remove them until they had exacted the full retribution for the massacre of Cawnpore.

Pressing on with all possible speed Havelock's relief column fought its way into the Residency. The first that the defenders knew of its approach was the sound of a royal salute of guns fired by approaching troops 16 miles away and the sound of the bagpipes as the Force came nearer. Havelock's Force, however, was not strong enough to free the defenders of Lucknow and although a great help in defence, their coming meant more mouths to feed and food was very scarce. However, in spite of losses through smallpox, dysentery and cholera, the garrison held on until 17th November 1857. The city was finally relieved by a strong Force under Sir Colin Campbell, but Campbell decided to evacuate and one night, under the cover of darkness, the garrison marched away to safety.

The defence of Lucknow lasted 140 days; the 32nd Cornwall Foot Regiment having stood firm throughout and for the first 87 days, alone. The casualties suffered by the 32nd during the siege were 15 Officers and 364 other ranks dead, 11 Officers and 198 other ranks, injured. Figures for women and children are not recorded other than their sufferings.

Queen Victoria greeted the men, women and children on their return to Portsmouth to honour their courage. Lucknow, then became the only Embassy in the British Empire not to lower the Union Jack at dusk, in recognition of what was a unique, heroic and magnificent military achievement.

The name of Lucknow will ever be sacred in the annals of the 32nd Regiment, for even among the many gallant deeds recorded in the history of the British Army, the defence of Lucknow stands out from the pages of history in bold relief.

The Regiment became a Light Infantry, Commanding Officer Sir John Inglis was promoted and decorated; four members were awarded the Victoria Cross. Today, on Walker Lines Industrial Estate, Bodmin, site of the former World War II extension to Victoria Barracks, we have Lucknow Road. They are not forgotten.

Cock's Well

St. Leonard's Holy Well

Liskeard Road Toll House Well

Laying of public sewer

On the track of fever
Sewer contractor: believed to have been a very untrustworthy worker

North Cornwall has faced problems with its water supply in recent years. The 1800s saw action taken when fear stalked the county town.

In February 1882, when Mr Buchanan of the Medical Department received Dr Parson's report to the Local Government Board on Enteric Fever in the Bodmin Registration District, it represented an investigation Sherlock Holmes would have been proud of, being painstaking, thorough, and most importantly it pinpointed the cause and offered the cure. It was said by medical practitioners at that time that cases of typhoid fever occurred sporadically every year in Bodmin, but in 1881 with sixty cases and nineteen deaths, fear was brought into the borough. The time had come for an expert investigation and Dr Parsons was the man.

Over a hundred years ago the town numbered 5,061 people and contained several public institutions, the county asylum, the county gaol, the militia barracks, the union workhouse, and the East Cornwall Hospital. In the east of the town there was a network of streets and lanes occupying the low ground and from the centre, roads radiated in all directions and houses rose in more or less scattered arrangements upon the slopes. The main thoroughfare, Fore Street/Bore Street had its subsidiary streets, narrow and crooked, many houses having no back areas and a good many devoid of any ventilation.

The sewage disposal arrangements left a lot to be desired and were the cause of many complaints. Plans for the sewerage of the borough were prepared in 1872 by Borough Surveyor, Mr Coom and work commenced in 1873. This was completed in five years, running east to west, to terminate just outside the town, onto irrigation fields, but appeared to overflow into the town leat polluting it to such a degree that townspeople found their favourite walk to Scarletts Well taken at a faster pace than they would normally have wished, and of course, when the wind was in the west the whole town suffered.

The distribution of the fever appeared through the following locations: Fore Street, Bore Street, side roads and the lower area of Pool Street and Mill Street, but the eastern portion of the town escaped. Also, the sufferers on the whole appeared to belong to the labouring or artisan classes, but here a problem arose with the investigation as a patient could be in the habit of working in a different area of the town to that in which he would sleep.

Suspicion fell on the water supply from the water company who, in dry weather, took their supply from Dunmere, just above the entrance of the town leat. Here it was pumped by water wheel to a reservoir at the west of the town 400 feet above sea level, (Dunmere is 62 feet above sea level), where this water was mixed with water from the Butterwell, a small moorland stream. The service was never constant and it was switched off periodically, on top of which it was never filtered before delivery. The good doctor found the water very turbid, samples of a very uninviting appearance were shown to him, and this only encouraged people to resort to springs and wells which yielded a clearer, more palatable brew but probably less wholesome beverage, in particular Church Stile, Bree Shute (Eye Well) and Cock's Well and in the upper town Bore Street and St Leonards, plus several pumps over wells.

Having received a report from the Medical Officer of Camelford that stated "Yes, we do discharge our sewage straight into the River Camel, but we have had no cases of fever this year" - the town's water company received an almost clean bill of health.

The milk supply was next to be ruled out. There were twenty two dealers in various parts of the town and each householder commonly resorted to his immediate milk seller in his neighbourhood and no fever had been reported in any milk seller's family.

Suspicion now centred on the sewers. The contractor employed to construct the sewers is admitted to have been a very untrustworthy person and no adequate supervision was exercised over the execution of the work, although eventually the council did terminate his contract. The inhabitants of Mill Street and Pool Street, where fever had been very prevalent, obtained their water from Cock's Well and Bree Shute (Eye Well). Having found out that three men who suffered worked as blacksmiths at shops near to Cock's Well and lived outside the borough, Dr Parsons ordered the source of the spring to be uncovered. This was found to be a small cavity under the road and within four feet of it and on a higher level, a sewer was exposed with leaking joints and the earth around sodden with sewage. Bree Shute (Eye Well) issued from the same strata a hundred yards along and was just as bad.

The same applied to the Town Wall pump which was situated in a recess of the wall and was said to have "improper use" made of it by passers-by and tramps in a common lodging house close by. This well served Bore Street and Downing Street. (There is more on this well but propriety must rule the day, suffice to say it was pretty awful from what I read).

The Borough Council took action by flushing the sewers and distributing disinfectant with printed directions for its use. Where a household had no direct flushing, a hose was directed into the bowl etc. Mr Derry was appointed Medical Officer of Health and Mr W J Jenkins, Inspector of

Nuisances, whom Dr Parsons regarded as an able officer, but underpaid, as there was no borough surveyor at that time. The Inspector of Nuisances superintended the execution of all public works carried out, he was also paid 3 shillings (15p) for each house with sewers. The borough council accepted the doctor's report and followed his recommendations regarding the water supply in Bodmin. The Sanitary Authority took steps to ascertain the condition of the sewers in their district. Particulars of rainfall at Bodmin furnished by Commander Liddell,

1881: January: 2.24" rainfall – 17 wet days; February: 7.52" - 18 wet days; March: 5.96" - 17 wet days; April: 1.95" - 13 wet days; May: 1.78" - 10 wet days; June: 5.95" - 22 wet days; July: 3.30" - 17 wet days; August: 4.84" - 24 wet days; September: 2.03" - 1-2 wet days; October: 5.08" - 14 wet days.

These simple particulars tell it all. When the heavy rain came in a month so the incidents of fever rose, with the dry spells they all but disappeared, but it took the able doctor to pinpoint the cause and offer the cure.

A cartoon of that period stated "a million insects in every drop." Such was the general confidence in every day drinking water in Britain at that time. But for residents in Bodmin the water from St Guron's Well that issues through the gargoyles at the foot of the churchyard steps proved to be a dependable source. Quiller-Couch spoke of it as "night and day, in the driest and hottest seasons, ever flowing, it serves the people with crystal water. A side trough refreshed the passing cattle and it lays the dust of Bodmin streets. It rolls on with the Priory rivulet, through the valley, past Scarletts Well, to pay its tribute to the Camel at Dunmere."

The water from St. Guron's Well issues through gargoyles at churchyard steps

WHJ

William Robert *'Budley'* Hicks (1808-1868)

William Hicks: Humorist was held in high esteem for enlightened and kindly work

Humour in old courtroom

Let us look back at a well-known figure of his day, renowned speaker, raconteur and wit, William Robert Hicks, who was born in Bodmin in the year 1808 and died in Bodmin in 1868.

A humorist yes, but also a man held in high esteem for his work in public life. He was born the son of a schoolmaster, a profession he took up himself early in life, but later became governor of the county lunatic asylum (St Lawrence's) an office he held for twenty years.

William Hicks was a kindly man and his term as governor led to a much enlightened approach to the inmates, in particular one referred to as Daniel, whose sayings, via a Hick's story, found their way into *'Punch Magazine'*.

A truly delightful retort to a friend of Hicks who said to Daniel: "Daniel, your hair is getting very white."

"Blossoming for another world" was the immediate answer.

Service was conducted at the asylum chapel by a clergyman whose character was certainly not of the best. Daniel stood waiting for the chaplain, and on his coming out said he wished to speak to him. The chaplain readily consented, and asked him what he wanted to say. Daniel began "Look here, Mr, I can't make you up no way."

"Why not?" said the chaplain.

"Why" replied Daniel, "because it seems to me, you serve the devil six days a week, then you come here 'pon the seventh, and abuse your best friend."

Hicks was a fine musician and player of the violin. Daniel took up the subject of music with him questioning the value of it. Hicks gave his opinion that it was a good thing and made people more refined. Upon which Daniel said *"I knowned a man that played the fiddle and he said, 'music hath charms to zooth the zavage beast' and he went into the field to play the fiddle to a wicked bull. I stopped outside to zee an end o'rt. The bull no zooner heard the scraping than he went vor'n. The man, he run to the stile for bare life. The bull got up to 'un just as he reached the stile and he took his fiddle and he gave the bull a back handed swipe across the norze (nose) with 'un, which scat the fiddle all to bits. There goes two-and-thirty-and-zixpence sez I."*

There are many stories concerning Daniel, but let us now take a more topical note, the Assize Court in Bodmin where a horsey looking gentleman was getting into all sorts of difficulties.

The witness was an ostler, and he said he was in the stable yard by himself at work, when the man who sold the horse came in. He had given evidence and was being cross-examined by the counsel, who wanted the exact words that were used in the conversation that took place between the witness and the man who it may be supposed, was the defendant.

Counsel *"You were in the stable yard at work and the defendant came in. Well what then?"*

Witness *"When I zeed 'un come in, I ses, ses I, 'how about the horse?' and he zaid he'd give me ten shillings to zay nothing about 'un."*

Counsel *"He did not say 'he'd give you ten shillings"?*

Witness *"Yes a did; that's xactly what a did zay."*

Counsel *"He could not have said 'he' he must have spoken in the first person."*

Witness *"No. I was the first person that spoke. He comes into the yard and I ses, ses I, 'How about the horse?' and he zaid he'd give me ten shillings to say nothing about 'un."*

Counsel *"But he did not speak in the third person."*

Witness *"There was no third person present. Only he and me".*

Counsel *"Cannot you tell me the exact words he used?"*

Witness *"Zo I have, I've a told 'ee".*

The judge now entered the fray.

"Listen to me, witness. He could not have said 'He' would give you ten shillings to say nothing about it; but 'I' will give you ten shillings".

Witness *"He said nothing about your Lordship. If a zaid anything about your Lordship, I never heard 'un. And if there was a third person present I never zeed 'un".*

There was uproar in the Court and the Judge and Counsel gave up in despair.

Hicks heard Counsel a witness ask if the prisoner had been drinking.

The witness replied *"He was a little as regards to liquor."*

"What do you mean by that?"

"Torsticated".

A young counsel was examining an elderly Cornishman who was a witness in court and raising a laugh at the expense of the witness. He said to the witness *"Well, what do you do?"*

"I keep a beer house".

"Where?"

"Jist out o' Bodmin."

"Whereabouts?"

"Nigh the Pound" (near the Cattle Pound).

"Oh nigh the Pound, eh? Then you sell beer by the pound?"

"Well, I do, as you may zay and I don't, as you may zay."

"Oh, that's a curious answer! You do, as you may say and you don't, as you may say. How do you do, as you may say?"

"Very well, thank you, how be you?" was the prompt reply.

The witness had set his trap, into which the young counsel had fallen, the laughter was on the other side and echoing all round the court.

©WHJ

A tribute to Mr Harry Dennison

We should today, remember with gratitude, a young man who, in January 1907, left Bodmin for Canada, an exciting new life ahead of him, but who would never forget his native town.

Perhaps like me you enjoy Priory House, for its elegance, the grounds for leisure and sporting facilities, perhaps you walked or drove along Bodmin's busy through road to reach them. All three have a common link.

T H (Harry) Dennison was born in Bodmin in 1886 to become an apprentice plumber with George Garland & Son. After the completion of his apprenticeship he emigrated to Canada, setting up home in Toronto. Mr Dennison's attitude to emigration was summed up in his own words *"I never had any regrets at leaving England. Anyone who has the will to work will, eventually, improve their position"*. Harry Dennison lived up to that statement, he prospered in Toronto and was highly esteemed in that city, but always retained a keen interest in the happenings of his native town.

It was following a visit in 1953 that he donated the splendid wrought iron gates at the entrance to Priory House and grounds.

These were dedicated on Coronation Day and are a permanent memorial of the Coronation and perpetuation of the memory of his family.

Coronation Day started early with one a and a half hour peal by the bells of the Parish Church, composed by one of their number, Mr J Riddle. It incorporated 272 changes and the ringers were led by 62 year old Mr Richard Sandy, celebrating his Golden Jubilee as ringer.

In 1957 a local newspaper stated the need for a new sports grandstand. Mr Dennison, who had the '*Guardian*' posted to him, undertook to pay for it and in September 1958 he and his sister, Maude, formally opened the new £2,500 grandstand, which seated 450 people.

After the ceremony, Mr Dennison saw a Cornwall County Team defeat a Bodmin side 8-1. The turf consultants who were advising the Town Council on the preparation of the new No 1 pitch, adjoining the new grandstand, gave permission for this one match to be played there but the pitch would not be in regular use until the following season.

Only six days before the opening of the grandstand the Council specially convened to admit as Honorary Freemen of the Borough of Bodmin: HRH Prince Chula Chakrabongse of Thailand, GCVO, Princess Chula Chakrabongse and T H Dennison Esq.

It was a colourful ceremony, unusual in that an eastern Prince, Prince Chula and English wife, Princess Elisabeth who made their home at Tredethy, near Helland, joined Mr Dennison, who was born in Bodmin, but made his home in Canada, in receiving from the Mayor, Mr T S Hore, this tribute of the Borough's esteem and gratitude. Prince Chula was frequently visited at Tredethy by his cousin, top international racing driver, Prince Bira. Both princes were the great grandsons of King Mongkut of Siam, subject of the film '*The King and I*'. The Chakrabongse arms can be seen on the front of Narisa Hall and bandstand, Priory Lawn, and were presented to the town by Prince and Princess Chula in 1957.

Sadly, though, it was in February of the following year, that news reached Bodmin of the death of Mr Dennison; tributes poured in from every quarter. The Town Council, then received news that in his will a further bequest to the town of Bodmin of £1,000 was to be kept invested for the town, the income to be used for charitable purposes. The fund was to be known as '*The Dennison Family Christmas Fund*'.

At the May 1959 Council meeting it was decided upon completion of the Downing Street area, it should be re-named Finn V C Estate, and the new relief road be re-named Dennison Road. As a number of people had suggested Dennison Road, a draw was made and Mrs E Scantlebury of 12, Berrycombe View was to be the guest of the Mayor at the official opening. John Yates, 18, Crockwell Street who suggested Finn V C also joined them.

At the opening, the wife of Bodmin MP Douglas Marshall referred to the lamented death of Mr Harry Dennison so soon after his visit to Bodmin the previous year. It was a shock to them all, but his courage in building a new life in Canada and his generosity to his native town would be commemorated for ever in the name of the new road. *"This road becomes a link between this ancient Borough of Bodmin and the great dominion overseas,"* she said.

For the sincere benefactor who never forgot his native town, may those words ring ever true. On a recent visit from Canada accompanied by his wife, Susan, Mr Foster Dennison (nephew of the late T (Harry) Dennison) presented Mrs Maureen Tooze, Curator of Bodmin Town Museum, with a cheque for £1,000. Mrs Tooze expressed her thanks on behalf of the Museum for this generous gesture and for the kind interest that Mr Dennison has always shown in the Museum, which has been greatly appreciated. Peter Davies, Museum President, stated, *"This substantial donation will enable our archival studies to be greatly improved for the benefit of historians and residents alike. We always seek to improve our standards of service and conservation. This will be of tremendous value within our aims and objectives. We are truly appreciative."*

Mrs Susan Dennison, Mr Foster Dennison and Mrs Maureen Tooze

HOWARD 1212
TELEX: 22837.

TELEGRAMS:
"BELLING, ENFIELD."

YOUR REF.

BRIDGE WORKS, SOUTHBURY ROAD,

ENFIELD,

MIDDX.

DIRECTORS
C. R. BELLING (GOVERNING)
R. M. HAWKINS
D. M. BRUNTON
H. P. ASTON
C. E. BELLING
R. P. DEAN
G. K. COLDWELL

OUR REF.

March 1963

Dear Sir,

     I would be very pleased if you would accept the
enclosed book which, as a matter of fact, has been produced
chiefly for our employees in celebration of our Golden Jubilee.

     Although it deals mainly with the history of this Company
over the past 50 years, I think it may also give some idea as
to how the Domestic Appliance side of the Industry as a whole,
has gone ahead in that time and, in fact, kept well in line with
the expansion of the Electrical Industry generally.

         Yours sincerely,

C. R. Belling.
Governing Director.

**Letter sent to Bodmin Town Museum from Belling & Co. Ltd. Signed by
the Governing Director & Founder, Mr Charles R Belling.**

From Clocks to Cookers – A family affair

This month we discover how a grandfather clock became an electric cooker and a Bodmin family of many generations became a household name. The earliest recorded mention of a clock in Cornwall is 1432 AD which can be found at St Mary's Church, Launceston. A primitive affair, no doubt, but it introduced mechanised time into our lives. Although dawn and dusk were of importance, so now tentatively no doubt was the time in between.

Let us go back to 1706 when a certain John Belling started a business in Fore Street, Bodmin, making and selling clocks to the local families of large farms and mansions, who would request a striking clock, whose sound could be heard throughout the house. For the poorer, would-be clock owners there was a clock hire service, because time was becoming important as the 18th century wore on and Bodmin was to become one of the principal clock making towns in Cornwall, with the families of Belling, Broad and Arnold being the most prominent.

Belling was perhaps the best known clockmaker in Cornwall. He made many single handed clocks which were cheaper and of course could be understood by all, eight day grandfather clocks, 30 hour clocks and as the family continued to trade over two hundred years in Fore Street they became watchmakers and gunsmiths as well.

Examples of Belling clocks can still be found today; however, many original cases suffered through Cornish kitchens having a low ceiling. Rather than have the clock go up through the ceiling, a hole would be dug in the floor, which in itself created another problem, in that the case would, in time, rot away through damp.

To deliver the clocks in those early days, at times, required a certain courage and endurance, perhaps missing from today's buzzing delivery vans, although the following was surely beyond the norm. Two men carried a grandfather clock for 12 miles over Bodmin Moor, around the bogs, skirting the marshy bottoms to reach the lonely farmhouse, watched by wondering sheep, whose only interest in time was dawn and dusk. After all their efforts one can only hope that the farmer was at home when they arrived.

The sales were not always cash sales; a Mr Parnell paid one guinea and twenty one pounds and three ounces of black tin valued at eight pence per pound towards a clock with further payments in tin later. But one can see from a little jotting book he carried at that time that perhaps payment was made in other ways. On Thursday 10th September 1751 he notes he has "two bottles of French Brandy in ye cupboard conseal'd" and others were hidden away at various dates up to the following March.

Belling Lantern clock, made in 1753, an example of the fine workmanship of John Belling. It is an alarm time-piece with a 30 hour movement and is almost unique. © *WHJ*

Taken from a newspaper of the day 1936; *"Seated at his workbench at the back of his window, with his lens adjusted to his eye, there could be seen day after day, seventy years ago, a clever workman in the person of John Belling, watch and clockmaker. His survival was of the old type of practical workers in the art of watch and clock making. The shop possessed an old fashioned bow window and it was situated just opposite the top of Chapel Lane. The window was not garnished with a display of watches and jewellery like the shops of the present day, but the walls of the shop were covered with clocks of all descriptions and several of the grandfather clocks stood on the floor. The shop also dealt in guns and fishing tackle".*

John Arnold was born in Bodmin in 1734 and was apprenticed to his father who was a watchmaker. As a young man he went to London as a journeyman, had little success and then went to Holland for a few years. On returning to London he set himself up in business in London specialising in very fine and small work. He made a small repeating half-quarter watch, mounted it on a ring and presented it to King George III in 1764. This masterpiece was only one third of an inch in diameter and had 120 parts. For this elegant example of his craftsmanship the King presented Arnold with 500 guineas and his career was established. Later being financed by a share of £10,000 granted by an Act of Parliament, he made a chronometer which Captain Cook took with him in the Resolution on his second voyage in 1772. In 1778 John Arnold and his son established a chronometer manufactory at Chigwell, Essex.

The twenty first century continues the tradition of clock making in Bodmin with the company of Richard Broad. Founded in 1972 they manufacture reproduction clocks to the highest quality and in using the name Richard Broad, they ensure that the name of one of Bodmin's clock making families is not forgotten.

There is an excellent little book by Canon Miles Brown on Cornish Clocks which is well worth a browse and here I quote the last paragraph; *"They have shared the hours of gladness and pain, the events of birth and death, the rise and fall of family fortunes; they have been inherited, bought and sold. They have served each owner with the same fidelity and impartiality until they have become part of the lives of the Cornish people".*

Charles R Belling (1912)

But what of the electric cooker? Well, Mr Charles Belling, born in Bodmin in 1884, left as a young man and in 1912 founded the company Belling Electrical. It was very much a one man and his boy concern, operating from a small shed tucked away in Enfield, manufacturing electric heaters. In 1922, Charles Belling, went into partnership with Edgar Lee, forming Belling and Lee Limited, and in 1932, they started working with John Logie Baird and, by 1938, they had installed the world's first community television system in Bentall's department store in Kingston-upon-Thames. Today, Belling Electric Cookers are known throughout Britain and Europe.

Mr Richard Belling, Managing Director of the company, cousin of Mr Charles Belling paid a personal visit to Bodmin Town Museum in 1990 and was presented with a book about the Belling family history in Bodmin. In return he gave a book of the first fifty years of Belling Electrical.

So in that joint gesture we have travelled from grandfather clocks to electric cookers in three hundred years.

Temple Church in the May sunshine

Knights Templars

How many of us who cross Bodmin Moor spare a thought to the small parish of Temple sitting astride the old coach road, hidden away from the bustling traffic of the A30. It can, in today's noisy world, slumber in peace.

Knight Templar

Temple takes its name from the Knights Templars, a military and religious order founded in the year 1118. The Knights established churches and hostels all over Europe for travellers and it is thought they built the church and hostel at Temple to accommodate travellers crossing over the wild and dangerous moor.

In later history the church, dedicated to St Catherine, was described as the Gretna Green of Cornwall, as it was a place where marriages could be performed without banns or a licence. The 16th century historian, Carew, described it "as lying in wild wastrel exempted from the Bishop's jurisdiction, where many a bad marriage bargain is yearly slubbered up, and, with parsons in receipt of their grateful donations." This came to an end in 1753 when an Act was passed declaring such marriages illegal and as a result the church fell into disuse. It lost its passing congregation and without doubt a more than fruitful source of income from runaway couples who escaped across the moor.

By 1784 the moorland weather had caused havoc. The church roof collapsed, falling timbers taking the life of a sheltering tramp, whose bones were later found beneath the ruins. The church was desolate with an immense ash tree growing from the nave. In 1850 the Reverend Edward Steele of St Neot held a service in the ruins and started a fund for its rebuilding. Silvanus Trevail, a highly respected Cornish architect, prepared plans, free of cost, and in 1883 the Church was opened and consecrated by the Bishop of Truro. Over two thousand people attended, all was now forgiven.

The little church set down the hillside, its squat tower just peeking up enough to be seen from the road and facing out over wild moorland is just as it should be. How grateful travellers must have been to find this safe hostel when crossing the moor. The stained glass windows in the tower have always been a favourite with me and all the more pleasing to find that the north window - a Knight Templar on horseback - was given by Messrs Garland & Son of Bodmin.

Temple is in the Blisland Parish and surrounded by its industrial heritage. Tin streaming and mining took place across the moor to Warleggan for many centuries. One mine was known by the delightful name "Wheal Whisper". A small elvan roadstone quarry just in from Temple crossroads was worked for the Council up until the 1930s. It employed a number of local men and has a small cheesewring rock formation overlooking the quarry. However, it was china clay that would make an impact on the landscape. This was reflected in Temple's population - 12 in 1861, increasing to 36 in 1871. By 1874 consideration was being given to a railway - "The Temple Minerals Railway." Today, when we look at how difficult it must have been to take the china clay, for example, from the early Hawks Tor workings, by horse and cart to Padstow, we can immediately see the attraction of a railway. Within the parish, Glynn Valley Clayworks began pumping china clay by pipeline to Bodmin Road (Parkway) in 1920 where dries had been built along the railway sidings. The china clay was not of the top quality and today there are no pits operating on the moor.

The new turnpike from Bodmin to Launceston commenced in 1769 taking coaches through Temple. Here it was joined just above the church by the Liskeard to Camelford Packhorse route. The turnpike through Temple was not popular as it was very hilly and difficult and so a new road was built to the west. Could this have been Cornwall's first bypass?

The population of Temple has always been small in number but on one occasion the situation was dire - the whole of the male population was once hung for sheep stealing! Then we find out "the whole of the male inhabitants" were only two.

Prior to the D-Day landings in France the moor around Temple was under heavy use, particularly by the American services with troop carriers, tanks and jeeps carrying out exercises. It is still said that there are many army vehicles at the bottom of Menacrin Marsh. One gentleman recollects the moorland being covered with upright wooden poles all the way into Bodmin, when a German invasion by parachute forces was thought to be possible. Temple did come under attack when a German plane chased by a Royal Air Force fighter plane machine-gunned the roof of Hill House. No-one was injured but the holes made by the bullets could be seen in the slates.

Today only Millpool Rifle range remains, extending towards Temple and serving as a reminder of those dangerous times.

The Temple Church is well worthy of a visit. Its simplicity of build, set within a moorland landscape has created a special place, a place we should cherish within our rural heritage.

Lost In the mists of time - Davidstow Airfield

Today the A39 is a much improved road, but rapidly changing weather can bring thick mist and driving rain off the coast leading to hazardous conditions, none more so than the stretch between Otterham Station and Camelford.

All the more reason perhaps to query the decision to site a major Class A bomber airfield high up on the northern part of Bodmin Moor. The topography of this area of the moor in relation to flying could be judged as somewhat extreme with Brown Willy at 1377 ft [420m] and Roughtor at 1311 ft [400m] looking down on the airfield sited at 970 ft [296m] this, together with the weather, made Royal Air Force Station Davidstow Moor very difficult for operations to be carried out.

With the Air Ministry guidance stating 600 ft. [182m] above sea level as maximum, one can only surmise that war time urgency led the men from the Ministry, who, having unfurled a map, spotted a flat area of moorland away from population but close to the coast into thinking that they had made the right judgement. However, it was war time, work got under way and on the 1st of October 1942 in heavy mist and rain the airfield was opened although not fully completed. The following day a mobile cooker arrived and arrangements put in hand to ferry water in tanks from Camelford. Over the next month the station bedded down quickly to operate under Coastal Command, becoming operational 5th November 1942. Three days later 18 B24 Liberators flew in, the United States Air Force had arrived. They went straight into action the following day, taking part in a raid on U-boat pens in France which were very well defended so most aircraft would receive damage from anti-aircraft fire. Further missions continued and in the New Year a Polish squadron arrived who, together with British squadrons, took a Coastal Command role on U-boat patrols and air sea rescue.

The social side of the camp began to take place with drama groups, keep fit activities, dances, which were very popular with local people, a boxing tournament – RAF Davidstow v RN and Marines Plymouth, no result recorded; November 23rd the North Cornwall Hounds met, and all ranks to participate for physical fitness, I am sure the Hunt brought out the best in them whatever they all got up to.

The poor weather played havoc and caused much frustration. For example in August 1943 the Air Ministry allocated a secret trial of rudimentary ground controlled approach (radar) but weather conditions at that time caused it to transfer to RAF St Eval. The irony of that decision surely could not be lost on anyone at that time.

As the war continued personnel strength had built up to 1,757, all ranks, some very far from home but contributing to the war effort in difficult conditions. In November the Commanding Officer reported that out of 30 days, 13 were unfit for operational flying. There was no flying immediately before Christmas and everyone was looking forward to the WAAF Christmas Dance on Christmas Eve, but news came through that the Home Guard had reported an aircraft had crashed on Brown Willy. A search party of the RAF Regiment located the aircraft which was a Dakota of the United States Air Force and all four crew were dead.

The Station ceased to be operational on 19th September 1944. The last squadron was posted to RAF St Eval and the station put on a care and maintenance basis, with diversion facilities which proved to be needed from time to time. It continued to be used by the RAF Regiment for training purposes until early October 1945 and finally closed at the end of that year.

Royal Air Force Station Davidstow operated for three years, seeing a mix of aircraft, from American Air Force to what now appears to have been a number of squadrons working out of the station during that busy war time period. A lot of credit has to go to the personnel who kept the station operating whenever possible and at times in extreme conditions.

One of the runways and perimeter track were used in the early 1950s for motor racing, but later two roads were built across the airfield. The shell of the air traffic control tower remains as a lonely reminder of World War II.

One of the main runways of the former Royal Airforce Station, Davidstow Moor. Roughtor appears in the background with Crowdy reservoir at the edge of the airfield.

Rough Tor - the perfect target

When the aircraft engines faded into the distance and Royal Air Force Davidstow Moor closed, one could have been forgiven for thinking that peace and tranquillity would have returned to this remote area of Bodmin Moor. Well yes, but we have to allow the anonymous man at the Ministry to look at his map and say, "We need an aircraft bombing range, I have just the place." It was 1945, peace may have been declared but armed services always have to remain in a state of readiness for the next conflict and training grounds were needed. Having said that the arguments against the use of Bodmin Moor were powerfully made and a lengthy debate took place, including a letter to 'The Times' from A L Rowse, All Souls College, Oxford. The eminent Cornish scholar requested in a letter to the Lords of the Admiralty to look at a one inch Ordnance Survey map of the Moor and they would see how crowded it is with "interest". Precious little of these sites of interest would remain after being treated to a course of modern bombing. Editors used their editorials to support the debate, the following is one such editorial:

Our correspondence columns have lately provided evidence that the Admiralty's proposal to acquire twelve square miles of Bodmin Moor for use as a bombing range has caused perturbation in Cornwall and elsewhere. In Monday's issue, a report from our Special Correspondent summarized the objections to this scheme. The truth is that Bodmin Moor is a very noble tract of country, giving a rare sense of space and freedom, and offering unusual opportunity for refreshment of the spirit. That the nation should be threatened with the loss of the finest upland scenery in Cornwall, including Rough Tor and the famous Brown Willy, which reaches 1,375 feet, at a time when the national need for recreation is more deeply felt than it has ever been is serious indeed. But Bodmin Moor, as Mr A L Rowse insists this morning, is also an area of great archaeological importance and promise. Among the monuments it contains are the stone circles of Stripple Stones, Fernacre and Leaze. On Rough Tor there is a complex of villages illustrating the development of our civilisation through 3,000 years, between the Bronze and Middle Ages, and there are remains of other settlements on the other tors. Many prehistoric sites still await and deserve scientific excavation. The whole area breathes an extraordinary sense of antiquity and is steeped in Arthurian legends. Moreover, to round off the tale of threatened assets, it is also the catchment area of the North Cornwall Water Board, and as our Special Correspondent has pointed out, the Board considers that the carrying into effect of the Admiralty plan would seriously affect the whole water supply distributed by that "body". The Ministry of Agriculture is also affected, for valuable sheep grazing land is involved.

All these were quite sufficient reasons for the conclusion that, in selecting Bodmin Moor as a bombing range, the Admiralty made an extremely poor choice and many earlier choices of areas for similar essential warlike purposes were no more suitable. This hand to mouth selection of practice grounds was indeed quite inadequate as a method. The fact is that this densely populated island cannot indefinitely furnish the space that is necessary for training in modern mechanical warfare of all kinds. The argument for Empire training grounds in territories which can offer wide tracts of genuine waste land grows stronger with every new development of the science of war. What is certain is that a very strong case will have to be put forward before any degree of approval can be won for the proposed desecration of a remarkable area in a county, to which, as it happens, the Navy in its long history has much cause to be grateful. Such a case has by no means been made out yet. There will be many besides the traditional "twenty thousand Cornishmen" who will want to know the reason why.

One area of the moor that did come under fire during the war period was High Moor alongside Brown Willy. The Americans took their huge artillery guns to the east side of the moor, Penkestle Moor, behind Colliford Lakes and also close to the Hurlers stone circles outside Minions. Precautions were taken during the American friendly fire; commoners were advised when to move stock out of danger, though true to say it did have its exciting moments. Of course it was war time, but launching huge shells eight miles over farmsteads and the A30 trunk road to explode close to Brown Willy, one would have thought held more than a hint of danger, however safe the precautions.

Part of the proposed bombing range looking from Shallow Water Common, centre Garrow Tor with Roughtor in the distance.

"A sorry affair at Jamaica Inn"

The young man had now returned, his army life finished. His right arm survived but was useless. He walked with an awkward limp but he thanked God he was alive, his future was in the good Lord's hands.

As a boy of barely eighteen years, he and several of his friends joined the regiment and left Cornwall. Today, he alone remained to visit parents and say how gallant their son had been. Not to say how truly terrible their lives became, how awful their deaths had been, how pointless their cause had seemed. No, it was for King and Country, the sacrifice had been supreme. The regiment, or what remained of it, was proud of its sons.

From his discharge at Portsmouth, he made a slow and painful journey to Launceston, where his luck deserted him. It was Christmas Eve, and as such, there were no coaches, no farmers' carts as he trudged along. When he reached Jamaica Inn, high on Bodmin Moor, the pale winter sun was setting. He was half frozen and his injuries were causing him nagging pains. Although he was not usually one for drink he decided that he would have a brandy to keep out the cold before he set off again in an effort to reach Bodmin early on Christmas morning.

The drink went quickly to his head and his injuries affected his actions. To some of the drinkers he was an amusing sight and as the evening progressed he paid for their entertainment until his money ran out. When the landlord suggested that he should continue his journey he gave a strangled cry of despair, ripped open his shirt, displaying terrible scars to his chest and arm and pulled the medal, so gallantly won, from a chain around his neck and threw it down the bar. "Take it, Landlord." he cried, "Take it, give my friends more ale to enjoy my company."

On this Christmas Eve, Jamaica Inn became strangely quiet. The moorland folk, who only a few minutes before, had drunk their fill and made foolish fun of the poor unfortunate huddled in the corner, now turned their backs to hide the shame and embarrassment they felt. The young soldier, who had spent all his money for their entertainment now lay back in a chair next to the huge fire with his uniform undone, spittle running from his mouth, tears coursing down his cheeks, and exhaustion etched in his face.

The lanterns cast a warm glow and the smoke was thick from the men's clay pipes, whilst outside the north east wind moaned and sighed, the inn sign squeaking as it swung to and fro. For the landlord, the evening had certainly taken a turn for the worst. "They should all be drinking fit to bust," he mused, "It's Christmas Eve, but right now tis like being at a funeral and that's no mistake." He poured out a large brandy, "Moses", he called out.

A small wizened character, with his felt hat over his long grey hair, waistcoat, moleskin trousers and spats, sidled, almost crab-like, to the bar. He looked, thought the landlord smiling silently, like the original Cornish pixie - if I put him in a cage I could do well in the summer.

"Moses," he repeated, "Get hold of that brandy, boy, find that fiddle of yours and turn this funeral into something like a half decent evening."

Before long all was forgotten, drunken laughter rang out, dice were thrown and Moses madly dashed across the strings with his bow. The landlord left the bar and lifting the young man placed him in a corner. 'There boy, you sleep it off," he murmured, "and may Moses's fiddle not send you to the devil himself."

The young man slept, oblivious to all that had happened. His befuddled dreams caused him at times to call out, his cry however, was lost as in battle, with the ever increasing din, as the evening wore on.

Near midnight the sound of carriage wheels was heard echoing on the granite outside and in came a tall military gentleman, his boots ringing out on the slate floor as he strode to the bar. For the second time that evening, the inn went quiet.

"A large brandy, Landlord," he ordered in a voice that commanded attention. "Certainly, sir, at once, sir," said the landlord turning to take a bottle down off the shelf. "Good God man, I will have none of that peat water," exclaimed the man. "Do you think I am the excise, out the back and sharpish, you have got something better, I'll be bound."

The landlord returned, his huge bushy beard masking the oaths being muttered and placed a large glass on the bar. The man held up the glass, sniffed it appreciatively, sipped it and turned to the landlord, "Excellent," he exclaimed, "I will not ask where that came from."

Slowly his gaze took in the room, while behind him the landlord waved frantically to Moses, who like others, had stood spellbound throughout the brandy episode. The young soldier awoke, had he been dreaming? Surely the voice he had just heard... he tried to stop thinking, his head started to spin again. "William Jago," shouted the man, "William Jago, my dear fellow." He strode across only to stop with a look of horror on his face. He returned, grabbed the landlord and led him to the end of the bar where everyone had now backed into a corner.

The silence was broken by a crash and a twanging sound as Moses dropped his fiddle and stood on it, bending down, his hat was taken off and thrown to the floor.

The man spoke, his voice shaking with anger, "I will not ask what happened here tonight," he said, "It is all too obvious to see. William Jago, for that is his name, was the bravest man in the regiment. I suspect you have seen his injuries. Now you have taken advantage of that young man, now you will pay. I expect to see money, to my satisfaction put on that hat." He pointed to Moses's hat lying on the floor. "As for you," he released the landlord, "you will clean up that boy, supply me with blankets and help get him into the carriage, and by the way, return anything your mischievous hands may have got hold of."

They left Jamaica Inn with the moon lighting their way, the carriage swaying along the turnpike, the two horses eager in the cold night air to be on their way. For William Jago, a new leather pouch with coins from Moses's hat, his medal from the landlord "and two gold coins on behalf of the regiment," murmured the man as he placed the pouch safely in William's jacket.

Dawn was breaking as the carriage reached the town. With care they descended Castle Hill and turned into Pool Street. As for the Jago family, their son had returned and their Christmas was complete. The Christmas star melted into the dawn of Christmas day, as the man turned the carriage for the now short journey to Priory House, also safely home for Christmas and pleased in the knowledge that the regiment had looked after one of its bravest sons.

A happy and peaceful Christmas to one and all.

Jamaica Inn, high on Bodmin Moor, made famous by Daphne du Maurier

BTM

Gawns Wheel, Durfold Meadow Pit, Bodmin Moor

The Gawns Wheel – a mighty attraction

It was a giant, traction engines had to haul it, local people walked miles to view it. But at the end of the day, was it one man's ultimate indulgence with his passion or did it have a practical use?

During the 1850s tin mining took place north of Blisland, not on a large scale but sufficient to warrant a smelting works and stamps for crushing the ore. However, they had a problem with stability, the ground held a lot of clay.

Within a few years Mr Frank Parkyn arrived, the son of a prosperous wool merchant from Lerryn. He was sent to live on the Moor because of his delicate health, this proved to be an astute move as he lived to the ripe old age of ninety. Mr Parkyn lived at Durfold Manor, near Blisland, and worked the adjoining Durfold Clay Works, one of the first China Clay works on Bodmin Moor and quickly went on to open pits around Temple.

Early production methods allowed for clay to be dried in the sun, but as methods improved drying works were built. It was convenient to dry the clay near to the pit but it incurred transportation difficulties in remote rural areas. Apart from cost, the carts did a lot of damage to the road surface, indeed by 1911 the tread of the cart wheel had increased from four and a half inches to six inches. To overcome this ongoing problem Frank Parkyn installed one of the first pipe lines to pump china clay direct to drying sheds built close to the railway near Tresarret in the valley of the River Camel beneath Blisland. The railway built to bring sea sand from Wadebridge for local farmers would take back china clay extracted from the moors above Blisland.

Working in the china clay dries (drying sheds), when coal was used for heating had its own hazards. For instance, snakes, namely adders, would be attracted by the warmth but the vibration caused by pushing wagons of clay across the shed would quite often dislodge a snake, dropping down on the unsuspecting workman underneath.

By 1919 Frank Parkyn needed to pump out clay from his clay pit at Temple. The action taken was quite staggering. He purchased from a mine in the Isle of Man a mighty fifty foot diameter water wheel. Even the journey was a feat in itself, for on arrival at Wadebridge it was brought to Blisland by traction engine and if you think of how narrow the roads are with steep hills and sharp corners, what a task!

To accommodate the wheel a pit nearly thirty feet deep was needed, this was cut through solid granite. Another task in itself and here the local family of Greenaway were found to be to the fore. Having assembled the wheel it now needed to operate the pump at Greenbarrow Works, Temple, one and a half miles away across the moor. As the wheel turned it pushed a series of flat rods mounted on supports over the moor under the A30 at mile post 6 from Bodmin, to pump out the china clay.

The system had problems. Indeed one gentleman had the equivalent of painting the Forth Bridge. His job each day was to heavily grease the rods and pulley wheels over the moor. The problem being the cattle loved the grease and licked it off. This in turn had its danger with their tongues often caught in a pulley wheel, also a flick of tail could prove to be a painful exercise.

In truth it was not really successful and later the wheel generated electricity, transmitting the current across the moor by copper cable fixed to the dismantled rods now placed upright in the ground. However, very little changed over the years, for one night all the copper wire was stolen.

The huge water wheel when working was a great attraction but it was not only moorland folk who travelled miles to see it. The late Baron Hony of Bodmin remembered as a young man, sitting on the rods out on the moor and travelling backwards and forwards.

The Gawns Wheel, as it was called, was at that time the largest working water wheel in Cornwall. Following removal in 1971, it languished sadly in disrepair at a museum in Wales. The wheel has since been refurbished and re-erected at Laxey on the Isle of Man as a tourist attraction. Was it ever feasible as it screeched and groaned its rods backwards and forwards over the moor, or one man's passion with water power, who now, can say.

This article was written at the time when Wenford Dries were being decommissioned after 100 years of receiving piped china clay from Stannon Pit, high up on Bodmin Moor. It is envisaged following decommission that the Camel Trail Recreational Route could be extended to Wenford beneath St Breward. Should this happen one would hope illustrated text boards would be erected to remember the role Wenford played in Bodmin Moor's production of china clay.

BTM

Tin streamers: a mixture of iron will and superstition and not a little smuggling

Men who tamed the moor

It could be said the most independent of all Cornishmen was the tin streamer. Working high on the moors in the wildest of country, he lived by his own efforts and relied on instinct with a knowledge born of generations.

He lived on the moor, quite often for a week, returning on a Sunday to see his family and stock up with provisions.

The houses they built from granite boulders and turf were around thirty feet long by twelve feet wide, provided with a broad chimney in one end and a wood corner that would hold a cartload of turf and furze, more than enough to do the cooking for a week.

Quite often between the fireplace and the end wall of the house a place was contrived to be entered from the wood corner that would be large enough to store at least a score of barrels, mostly brandy, besides other goods, which required to be kept dry during their brief stop in transit over the moor. When the wood store was full, no person could see the chimney-end wall was double thickness.

A low entrance doorway, no more than four feet high was made in the middle of one side wall and there were no windows as such, just holes left in the walls, likened by one observer to portholes in a ship. With planks fastened on stakes in the ground at the chimney end and straw rushes or ferns for bedding, they were snug enough on the wildest of moorland nights.

Many of the hardy old gentlemen from Bodmin and about, who often hunted on the moors in the winter would stop for the night, with tin piled at one end and a blazing turf fire at the other; good liquor, wild fowl and rabbits a-plenty. Oh, what stories would be told through the evenings!

No excise men liked to venture too often in the tin leats and bogs of Bodmin Moor and to placate them barrels were left in places far from the actual stock, this in a sense kept everybody happy, none more so than the local gentry and innkeepers.

The tin streamers of that period were very tall and broad men, of whom it was said by an old Cornish farmer, "They've got a nause like a spaniel dawg, they can most smell tin, I tell 'ee".

With their working-dress consisting of a striped blanketing shirt, with jacket and trousers the same and huge knee boots, plated with iron they looked, and were, a race apart.

With most of their speech still using words of the old Cornish language and working the streams and marshes in search of tin, in a similar manner as their ancestors, they were as much a part of the high moorland landscape as the tors and tumbled granite boulders around them.

Superstition was part and parcel of their life. Indeed it would be a strong or very indifferent person who would not be affected by spending a day in the remote areas of the moor, let alone in those far off days when the crossings of Bodmin Moor was a task not undertaken lightly and visitors were a rare event.

As a countryman I understand why the chattering of magpies, the ominous croaking of ravens or the howling of the dog can be taken as portents of disaster.

For instance, the old rhyme of magpies - One is for sorrow, two is for mirth, three is a wedding and four is death - but if the hearer spat towards these birds while uttering these words of destiny, the spell was broken and the charm dissolved. Living in such a remote area everything would have been relevant, from a flight pattern of birds to colours of flames in the fire, all would have had meanings to take notice of. Foolish, perhaps, or is it something we have lost who knows?

My father was always convinced he had solved how the witch on a broomstick entered folklore.

On crossing a field one evening, he put some lapwings to flight and one flew across the face of a full harvest moon with its beak, the tuft of its head and tail outstretched, together with its wild cry, it somehow rings true.

Ancient customs were carried through the generations. The streamers on the first day of March would send a young lad to the highest hillock of the work, allowing him to sleep as long as he could, the length of his siesta being the measure of the afternoon nap for the tinners throughout the ensuing twelve months. An odd custom, with March on Bodmin Moor far from agreeable for an afternoon sleep, if possible at all.

The first red letter day in the tin streamer calendar was Paul's Pitcher Day, (January 24th), it was marked by a very curious custom in the then mixed mining and agricultural town of Bodmin.

On the day before the feast of St Paul, the tinners set up a water pitcher at a convenient distance and pelted it with stones until it was entirely demolished.

The men would then leave work and adjourn into a neighbouring ale house, where a new pitcher, bought to replace the old one, was successively filled and emptied and the evening given up to merriment.

It is thought that this was generally upheld as an ancient festival intended to celebrate the day when tin first turned into metal, though one old streamer observed at that time there was open rebellion against the water drinking system enforced upon them whilst at work.

I prefer the first interpretation, it sounds the sort of festival that could be fun. Youths had a more unsavoury version and on Paul's Eve were seen to slink along the streets of Bodmin and hurl a pitcher, commonly stolen, and filled with unsavoury contents, into any house where the door had been incautiously left open.

Tin streamers altered the face of the moor.

© PD

83

Tretoil Mine

Bodmin Town Museum

"Queen Victoria ran like a Billy and skipped like a lamb!"

Looking south from Bodmin Beacon, with the tall granite obelisk behind us, it is hard to visualise a mining landscape in what is today Lanhydrock golf course and attractive farming settlements.

From the Beacon looking slightly to the left of the hamlet of Kirland we see the mining stack of Tretoil Mine standing in the centre of three other mines namely, Wheal Messer, Blackheath Mine and Tregullon, all profitable and working around 1830 until 1860 producing over 30,000 tons of copper ore together with, in the last four years of production, 8,000 tons of iron ore from Tregullon.

Moving around clockwise, high on the facing hillside, midway between the road to Fenton Pits (here you would have found the Miners Arms Inn) and Reperry Cross is Wheal Mary Louise, now blanketed with scrub. Tin was excavated by a deep open cast working as well as by an adit entrance to the mine.

Continuing to the right, the next to catch our eye is Mulberry Hill, looking much higher than its 441 feet.

This area had been worked for centuries long before records were considered necessary, yielding 6 to 7lbs of tin to the ton and excavated to a depth of between 80 feet and 120 feet by 300 yards long. It was already a feature of the landscape in 1748 when Thomas Martyn published his map of Cornwall. This area is dangerous with a sheer pit and a high population of adders, you have been warned! I did witness a buzzard fly up with an adder when at Mulberry. The adder was released at some considerable height to drop down to the road below, collected again by the buzzard for a leisurely meal elsewhere.

A former prominent landmark from the Beacon is the now Cornwall County Council Re-Cycle Centre, Wheal Prosper, which ran alongside the old coach road out of Lanivet; an enormous pit measuring 50 feet deep by 300 yards long. During its working life it has been estimated over 2 million tons of rock must have been removed, yielding 3 lbs of tin to the ton.

The ore passed through a tunnel under the coach road to the dressing floors above Lanivet. The final operation took place in 1930 and had the last stamps to be erected and worked in Cornwall for crushing the ore-bearing material.

The pit was filled with household rubbish in the 1980s at an alarmingly fast rate. So, it is perhaps with a sense of irony that it today houses the major re-cycling centre.

The parishes of Lanivet and Withiel were in a heavy mining area in the 1800s, hard to believe today, but nature and time are great healers. Mining was also carried out in the Nanstallon and Boscarne areas without any long-term success.

Moving on around to the north side of Bodmin we find the Penbugle and Lancarffe Consuls in operation at Clerkenwater in 1845, engaged in the mining of lead under several companies, production ceased in 1853.

To complete the circle, you can follow the forestry walk in Cardinham woods to the silver mine thought to have been started in Roman times. The shaft goes down to over 360 feet deep.

To finish a report in the words of the mine captain of a visit in 1846 of Queen Victoria and Prince Albert to Restormel Mine, near Restormel Castle, Lostwithiel: 'I received a letter one evening from Mr Edmund to say as how Prince Albert was coming to our main (mine) the next morning. In the morning sure 'nuf we see the chay coming and who should be in it but the Queen as well as the Prince. The Queen got out of the chay and ran about in the wet grass like a Billy! Mr Taylor says to me "Is it safe for the Queen to go in the main?" "Safe", says I "tes as safe as the Rock of Gibraltar." So the drams (trams) was brought forth and some straw throwed into one and some green baize after it and the Queen skipped in like a lamb and I do believe that I touched her. She didn't like it tho', when 'twas wet, but when we came as far as we cud to the west lode, the Prince took the pick and he thrawed like a man! And he got a piece of ore.

"This," said he, "is from the west lode, so I put un in my left pockat, and then we went to the east lode so I puts un in my right pockat," he says. As they was a-coming out, says the Queen to Mr Taylor, "What's that there blue that I did see?" "Bless ye mam," says he "that's the light of day."

One hundred and twenty miners were ready to cheer 'em as they drove off (as red like injians from the red ore of the main) and did we cheer to be sure, as never was before.'

Please heed the warnings - all mines are dangerous places and permission to visit will need to be obtained from the landowner concerned.

Recommended reading, a far safer course of action, *'Mines and Miners of Cornwall'* by A K Hamilton Jenkins and your local Ordnance Survey Map, plus, of course, a visit to the Bodmin Beacon.

"A story for Christmas"

© PD

The marriage of John Yeo and Morwenna Pascoe brought two moorland communities together "us'll face the world together" said John Yeo Snr., glowing red in the face as he stood and addressed the wedding guests, "That's all I got to say" and promptly sat down to warm applause.

"Father never was a man for words" whispered John to his bride "unless he's dealing at market, then you cannot shut him up". Here he was interrupted by the final toasts to the bride and groom followed by the announcement "Your coach awaits you Mr & Mrs Yeo". The happy couple slowly made their way to John's well groomed horse and freshly scrubbed cart to journey across the moor, with Morwenna leaving Cardinham for a new life in St Breward Parish as the wife of John Yeo of Pengarrow Farm, in the very heart of Bodmin Moor.

John represented the fifth generation of Yeos to farm Pengarrow, inheriting the farm on the day of his marriage, "got to give the boy his chance" said John Snr., "Me and the wife have a little place in St Breward to settle back a bit."

For John, good summer grazing on Shallowater Common and winter grazing on Pengarrow, together with occasional quarry work, meant in three years the taking on of nearby Shallowater Farm. The future looked so good, solid stone hedges, gates well hung, the bottom two pastures looking lush, worth the sweat and toil of spreading the sea sand and Morwenna expecting their first child. "It will be a boy" said John "every first born Yeo is a boy." "It will be a boy, that's true," Morwenna agreed, "because he kicks so much at night."

"John," he was awakened from his thoughts, "John come quickly". Mrs Nankivell stood in the farmhouse doorway, her face creased with worry. A cry came from the house that set his senses reeling again, a cry that threatened to tear his heart apart, for Morwenna had now been in labour for nearly twelve hours. When the pains started he had ridden as arranged to fetch Mrs Nankivell at neighbouring Fox Tor Farm and she had been at Pengarrow Farm ever since. "Make sure we have plenty of furze, peat and water from the well, John, and you will be a father in no time at all" were her words on arrival, but now he pushed her aside and entered the house, the warmth from the fire, the aroma of cooking and steaming kettles seemed wrong in a house where his wife lay dying. Morwenna, now very pale and drawn reached for his hand, "please John, the child" she gasped, as a spasm of pain jerked her head back.

Mrs Nankivell took him to one side "Now John, you saddle up old Major while I pack you a pasty and something to drink, then set off right away because I don't like it. The baby ain't comin' and Morwenna's life is draining from her, you must ride to Bodmin and get Doctor Thomas. God bless him."

"Major, old son its a lot to ask of you, Bodmin and back" he muttered to the old horse as he adjusted the saddle, "so late in the day as well." He looked around, the sun was dropping fast and the mist was beginning to rise from the streams, later if the frost set in the mist would hopefully clear, but shortly he would have to rely on the horse to find its way.

"Hurry John" Mrs Nankivell cried "I will hang the big lantern in the porch to guide you from Menacrin Marsh". He rode off, cold and clammy, the mist closed in around him, the familiar landmarks lost, making his journey all the more perilous. He consoled himself, didn't his father say we Yeos grew from the peat itself, our blood runs black not red.

They climbed Hawks Tor coming out of the mist into a bright moonlit landscape, seemingly above the clouds with stars brightly sparkling. From nearby a fox barked a warning, they descended cautiously into the mist again, meeting an ancient track leading to a deep ford where old Major gratefully refreshed himself. John munched on his pasty and thought about finding a way through the tin streaming works that abounded in these parts for surely he could not afford his horse to go lame or take a tumble.

Setting off again they slowly headed for the turnpike and on rounding a hill both were startled to hear raucous laughter. A light from a tinner's turf hut could be seen, where no doubt a barrel of brandy had been broached, for smuggling across the moor was far from unknown. John began to get worried, the mist was playing tricks, a breeze had got up, swirling around. We could be going in circles, he thought, patting the horse's neck. He now kept to the bank of the stream before the works of the tinners forced him higher up the moor again. The old horse sniffed the air, he too could smell the rancid odour from Menacrin Marsh, the most dreaded and fearful of bogs on the whole moor. Only last year a farmer from Temple disappeared trying to save one of his cattle. Dear God, prayed John, keep us safe from Menacrin. They climbed again, now heading for the turnpike to Bodmin.

Unaware of the drama that would engage the family that evening the lights of 12 Castle Street, Bodmin were shining brightly and the household of Doctor Thomas was merry, for Christmas Eve meant the time when the servants and their families joined with the Thomas's in Christmas celebration. They filled the large sitting room with the family ensuring that every glass and plate was full. A log fire crackled in the hearth; it was a time of joy and happiness. "Come Mrs Bray, more plum pudding" enquired the kindly doctor's wife. "God bless you mam, if I eat another mouthful I swear I will never leave this chair till after Christmas and that would never do, me being your cook." "Time for carols" shouted out the doctor "now children I want the sweetest singing I have ever heard at Christmas." He sat down at the harmonium "now tell me your favourite carol."

The door bell jangled through the house setting the dogs barking and the children shrieking that it was Father Christmas, but all was silenced when John Yeo, half-frozen and mud spattered was led into the room. "Give the boy a glass of port." the doctor ordered. "William Bray, look to his horse". John went to speak. "No, boy, warm by the fire, get that port into you, then you can tell me what brings you to my house on Christmas Eve."

The room went quiet as his story tumbled out. He ended imploring the doctor to make the journey, fearing his wife would never see Christmas morning.

"Of course I will, my boy. William Bray, bring the horses around the front of the house. Mrs Bray, some food if you will and a flask of something strong, for this night will be long and the moor terrible and cold, and my dear wife, your prayers for that poor soul out at Pengarrow"

As they rode out of Bodmin, John spoke of the problems he encountered with the turnpike keeper at Callywith. "Leave him to me my boy" the doctor replied "he's always been a cantankerous old devil and Christmas Eve will not change him." "Russell, open up" the doctor cried out on arrival at the locked gate. A bedroom window opened a crack "damn ee I've gone to bed it's Christmas Eve". The window slammed shut. "Russell, you listen to me, you come down this minute and open this gate or by God I will never treat your gout again and that's a promise I will keep, you old devil." The doctor sat back on his horse. The door of the toll house creaked open to reveal the lantern carrying keeper "God sakes doctor, how did I know it was you sir, 'tis a terrible night for a journey. This weather plays up the gout terrible, sir". He hobbled to the gate, "Here" the doctor gave him a sixpence, "I will be coming back tomorrow so no more of your nonsense now." As they trotted away the doctor turned to John "To get Russell from his bed means we have overcome our greatest obstacle" he chuckled. "Come boy, let's see if that moorland nag of yours has anything left inside and get to that young wife of yours before dawn."

On leaving the turnpike near Temple the mist came in thick again. The doctor now quite fearful of losing his anxious companion urged his tired horse to keep up. Shortly John brought his horse to a halt as the stench of Menacrin Marsh filled their nostrils. "Doctor" said John, "we could be out here all night unless we cut through the marsh. Old Major will take us, we've struck the tinners' path but for the good Lord's sake stay close behind" John urged

Major forward not waiting for an answer for they both knew the risk they were taking. The haunting call of a curlew broke the silence. His horse cried out as the ground moved and trembled beneath them, their lives now completely bound up with their horses. They were skirting the centre as the path wound between clumps of scrub willow and stagnant pools. Suddenly old Major's ears pricked up, at the sound of running water, he broke into a trot. Even the rush of a startled snipe in his path failed to stop him. Within seconds they had crossed the stream onto open moorland, taking them out of the mist.

The flickering beam of a welcoming lantern could be seen in the distance. Tiredness slipped away from each rider and horse as they galloped, all eager to reach Pengarrow.

Inside the farm, Mrs Nankivell had been joined by her husband, Joss and together they did what they could to ease Morwenna's pain, for now she was very weak. Suddenly came the sound of horses. Joss rushed outside in time to catch Major's bridle as John leapt off, then helped the doctor to dismount. Doctor Thomas gathered himself together, patted Joss on the shoulder and strode inside. "Well Morwenna" he questioned "what problems have you got young lady?"

Sending John out wasn't easy but necessary to calm him and after a further difficult couple of hours Morwenna finally upheld the Yeo family tradition by bringing a bouncing baby boy into the world, whose cries fetched John bounding down the Tor. Doctor Thomas's skills had thankfully saved mother and child, both of whom slept peacefully and John and his friends now tucked into a large breakfast, "a Christmas breakfast" commented Mrs Nankivell.

A loud knocking at the door raised them from their thoughts. Outside stood two tall men, tin streamers who were invited in to join the breakfast table. The taller of the two stooped to pick up a small cask, explaining how they saw John ride by the previous evening and knowing his wife's time was due they suspected the worse and on seeing John return with the doctor through Menacrin, they realised their suspicions were right. "You were in the marsh" cried out Doctor Thomas. "Oh yes sir, we see everything and know everything on the moor. You were safe and so is the brandy, no excise man would attempt Menacrin Marsh, so here's a cask of brandy to wet the baby's head!" "So don'ee worry, doctor" said his companion "we will see'ee through to the turnpike when 'ee returns to Bodmin".

Morwenna stirred, "God bless you all" she murmured sleepily reaching out for her baby, "God bless you all for my Christmas child".

Out in the stable, two tired horses stood munching hay and gazing over the half stable door at the Christmas star which had been with them that Christmas night as it gently faded into the coming dawn.

A Happy and Peaceful Christmas to One and All

Unremitting toil gains reward

It was said an Englishman's home was his castle, well that being the case for many a Cornishman his home was his cottage, nothing more, nothing less.

Fishermen, miners, and farm workers built where they worked. For instance, when copper was discovered around Caradon, villages sprung up overnight, cottages one up, one down, erected by miners in the limited free time available to them.

In many parts of Cornwall the landowner would draw up a lease, dependant on 'lives' - a system where a leasee would lease a plot of land, erect a house on the understanding that at the death of the longest lived of three selected persons, the ground, together with all the buildings should revert to the original owner. In its day it was of immense value to Cornish landowners bringing thousands of acres of waste land into cultivation.

The following was discovered in an old report and is perhaps an extreme example of the system. It earned a certain Mr William Pearce, in 1804, a silver medal and fifteen guineas by 'The Society for the Encouragement of the Arts' for his unaided enterprise in reclaiming twelve acres of waste ground and converting it into highly cultivated arable land.

This gigantic and, as it would now appear, almost super-human task, was commenced by the man in question when he had already reached his fiftieth year and occupied no less than eighteen years of unremitting toil in bringing it to completion. During a considerable part of this time his circumstances were such that, so far from being able to employ labour, he was himself obliged to work for others during five days of the week, in order to obtain the one shilling (5 pence) a day on which he and his wife and a family of seven children subsisted. "As to the property," he wrote "when I first began this undertaking I had none, except one mare and the money which I earned in this way. I worked hard, however, for my employers in order to finish as soon as possible - not to leave off work, but in order to get home to start again at my own undertaking in improvement."

The land chosen for the purpose was unpromising enough to damp the ardour of any ordinary agriculturist, consisting as it did of a heathy swamp, its surface soil less than six inches in depth and beneath this a bed of loose stones, varying in size from a half a pound to three hundredweight or more. These circumstances rendering the use of the plough impracticable, the whole of the ground had first to be broken up by hand. This work in itself occupied a number of years, during which time the turf was removed and built up in piles,

91

the latter, when dry, being burnt and the ashes subsequently used for manure. Meantime, a start was made on the removal of the underlying stones which were carried to certain spots, in order to build the Cornish 'hedges'. No less than seventeen of the latter were erected in order to divide the property into the eight different fields or enclosures which were thought necessary for the various kinds of produce it was intended to grow. The ground, as already mentioned, being very swampy, had also to be intersected, with various drains, which emptied themselves into deeper ditches, which were dug round the margin of each field. These, indeed, served a double purpose, as thereby a greater height was given to the hedges. At every gateway a bridge capable of supporting a loaded cart was made over these watercourses. However, before the land could be cultivated, further supplies of manure, consisting for the most part of sea sand, had to be brought from a beach, the average annual quantity of the material thus used being fifty loads and the total distance travelled in fetching it, two hundred miles. In addition to this, at least another two hundred miles a year was traversed during part of the time in delivering coal, a supplementary occupation undertaken by the indefatigable leasee in order to eke out his slender livelihood.

At last, the time came when the land on which this incredible amount of labour had been spent actually reached the producing stage and in 1803, the proud farmer had the satisfaction of reaping ten Cornish bushels of barley, nine trusses of hay, two hogsheads of oats and ten bushels of wheat. "Having dealt with the ground, I began," he writes, "to erect a dwelling house on the spot, the walls of which were composed of turfs and the roof rafted and thatched by myself, although I was bred only to husbandry. To the other house I have added, as I was able, a barn, stable, cart shed and other convenient outhouses for my cattle, which at present consist of three horses and one cow, two heifers, two steers and one yearling, to which may be added as another part of my small stock, a few bushels of different grain and a wheelbarrow and other tools necessary for husbandry."

Such perseverance in the face of these difficulties would have been remarkable enough under any circumstances; but in this case it was rendered all the more astonishing by the fact that a physical infirmity to which the farmer was subject, necessitated the performance of the whole of the work, including that of driving the plough, solely with the aid of one hand.

Judged by every standard of common sense, even a medal and a prize of fifteen guineas, together with having his achievement recorded in a set of very pedestrian verses, would seem an inadequate reward for such a vast expenditure of toil, the fruits of which must in so short a time, have redounded to the benefit of another. Yet such was the temptation of getting a piece of land on which to erect a home of their own, that the system of leasing on lives continued throughout the whole of the nineteenth century to prove as attractive to the working people of Cornwall as it was profitable to the landlords.

It was a hard system, especially in the case of elderly women, who quite often were left homeless as well as husbandless, by the death of the last life.

Elderly Cornishman at home in the scullery

A very hard life, yes, but there was humour and I relate the following:

During an election the candidate spoke at length on the hardships of the "three life system" when a staunch supporter rose at the back of the hall to tell the astonished audience the following story.

Talking of the troubles of poor old widows, do put me in mind of what poor Betsy Lobb said to the Parson when he came to her when she were dying.

"Well goodbye passon" she said when he got up to go, "I do wish ee well! Seemen' to me, I shall soon be in Belzbub's (the Devil's) buzzum now!"

"No! No! Betsy," exclaimed the horrified Parson, "I do hope you're going to a far better place than that!"

"Naw Passon! Doan't ee wish me no better; I'm logen for to go to Belzbub's buzzum!" says Betsy again.

"Really now, Betsy" cried the now distraught Parson, "I hope you are mistaken, let us pray that it is Abraham's bosom you are bound!"

"Aw, Aber'm es et?" returned Betsy, "Well Passon, you do knaw more than I do 'bout they folks up above and I caan't tell but what you're right. But Belzbub or Aber'm tes all one to me; for I've been leven a poor lone widdy-wumman for nigh fifty year and so long as tes a man's buzzam I'm bound for, I don'y much keer!"

93

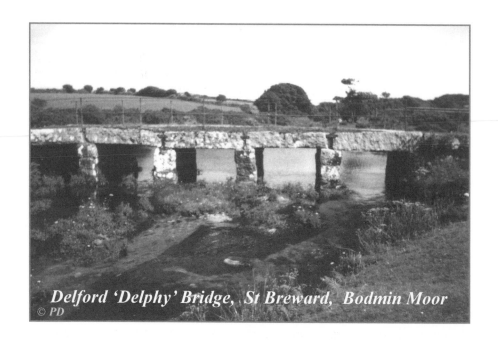

Delford 'Delphy' Bridge, St Breward, Bodmin Moor
© PD

Boundary Stone, Brockabarrow Common
© PD

Burning the candle at both ends

Having laid in the electricity supply, the engineer decided the following month to call and enquire how the elderly farming couple were getting on. "'Tis a marvellous invention" came the enthusiastic reply to his question. "Why, every night before we go to bed we can switch on that bulb and see to light the candles."

So, the farmer proved there was lighting before the Electricity Board, now let us now go back to before the farmer's use of candles.

The first form of lighting came from an earthenware lamp, shaped like a heavy candlestick, but having at the top, instead of a small socket for a candle, a well large enough to contain one or two cupfuls of oil. The edge of the well was provided with a lip in which rested the wick, at first made from the pith of rushes, later from cotton. Not a great deal of light, but an improvement on glowing embers of the fire.

Later, an iron version called a "chill" (Cornish for lamp) came in; this would hold more wicks and could also be hung from a wall. Both types used oil expressed from pilchards. Indeed, until the start of the 1800s, it was sold in Cornish towns as commonly as paraffin was until the mid 1950s. The oil was brought to market by fishwives in big jars and retailed to country folk who included it in their weekly purchases.

When it came to close work something better was required and here candles came in. Made from the pith of rushes and dipped in tallow, these being pliable and held in an iron stand, could be bent around. This, however, was thought to be an extravagant thing to do and from it arose the proverbial warning "burning the candle at both ends." Various improved candles came about but in reality never much of an improvement as the smeech (acrid smell) made equalled, if not exceeded the "odour" emitted from the burning of pilchard oil.

Of course, one had to light the early lamps or candles and this could be a long and tedious process because the people of Cornwall had to rely on tinder and flint. The tinder consisted of a piece of cotton rag which had been soaked in a solution of saltpetre and then dried. Sparks were produced by striking a piece of flint against steel, which then fell on the tinder, causing it to ignite. A very tedious process and if a light was suddenly required in the middle of the night one can imagine the frustration it would cause.

The matches of those days were, likewise, homemade. They consisted of thin strips of wood, five inches long, about a quarter of an inch wide, dipped in melted brimstone. When the tinder has been ignited, one end of the match was applied to it and the brimstone burst into flame.

Notwithstanding the laboriousness of the process the modern 'strike-a-light' matches were first regarded with considerable distrust. There was a certain lady of mature years who was presented with a sample for trial and being of a cautious turn of mind thought she should test them before going to bed. Accordingly, taking one up in her trembling hands, she struck it gingerly against the box, instantly a little blue flame appeared. "Ais, that wans alright" she muttered to herself, blowing it out carefully and replacing it before picking up another. The remainder proving satisfactory she retired to bed with an easy mind. Next morning, one of her neighbours inquired how she liked the new 'strike-a-lights'. "Why, my dear," was the reply, "they aren't no good at all. Come the middle of the night, when I wanted to see, not wan of they blessed matches would strike, for all they was right enough last night. No my dear, give me the ould tinder and flent, that'll see me to the end of my days I reckon."

So for the farmer and his wife there was lighting before the Electricity Company, the humble candle, and they felt comfortable and confident to continue a habit of a lifetime.

But for the old lady, who shrugged aside the new fangled matches, the farmer could only find use for the electricity to see to light his candles. On what I wonder will we be judged as our eccentricity, when future generations look back.

© Cornish Studies

A hazardous journey for Justice

Let us start with a simple premise:

The town of Launceston is the capital of the Duchy of Cornwall, the town of Bodmin is the county town of Cornwall and the city of Truro is the administrative centre of Cornwall.

BTM *Launceston Castle*

When Robert, half brother of William the Conqueror, built Launceston Castle the town became capital of the Earldom, then subsequently Duchy of Cornwall.

Launceston's importance was strategic and for that very reason it became the first county town simply because the roads into Cornwall were truly awful and hazardous. The judges, who by statute, had to hold sessions in principal and chief towns of counties, had no wish to travel further into Cornwall than was necessary and so Launceston fitted the bill and the rest of Cornwall suffered.

1715 saw a petition from JPs, gentlemen, freeholders and people of Cornwall to Parliament submitting that as Cornwall was 80 miles long and the courts were only one mile inside the border, many were debarred by age, infirmity, expense and hazard, from seeking justice. From this pressure came the sharing of the courts with Bodmin, but the judges had to find Bodmin, and hence the town had to pay a horseman ten shillings (50 pence) to ride to Polson Bridge, beyond Launceston, to meet the judges as they crossed into Cornwall to act as guide.

The 18th century saw a movement of population from the east to the west of the Cornwall and by 1750 Bodmin had lost its population lead; the mining boom was on. It became imperative that justice was easily accessible to everyone.

Christmas 1821 saw Reginald Carew Pole of Antony, who was Foreman of the Grand Jury of Cornwall, commence a move for the Assizes to be held in Bodmin. The Act was on the statute in 1836 for the building of new courts and providing judges lodgings; this, despite the efforts of Truro with a petition in 1833 that they be given the Assizes.

1837 saw the old Friary Church give way to the new Court House and the Mayoralty House, rebuilt as Shire House, the judges' lodgings. The then Borough Council built the Shire House which was rented to the justices and a caretaker or steward installed. The following year on 3rd July, the Shire Hall was opened for quarter sessions and on 28th July Her Majesty's Justice of Assizes held court in the new county town of Cornwall.

In 1967 Lord Parker of Waddington, during his first visit to Bodmin as Lord Chief Justice, was reported as having said that he hoped Bodmin would remain as Assize Town as in his opinion Bodmin was a perfect example of bringing law to the people rather than people having to go to the law; that of course, was the original grounds for removing the courts from Launceston.

However, in 1988, 150 years almost to the day of the court opening, Mr Justice Nolan was performing its closing ceremony. At a cost of approximately £4.2 million a new Assize Court complex had been built in Truro, a sad day for Bodmin and North Cornwall.

Let us look back on two cases where the judges were not happy with the Cornish jury system, when it came to decisions in Bodmin Assize Court:

The headline read "Judges Criticise Jury Verdict". At Cornwall Assizes, Bodmin, the accused had been found guilty of unlawfully wounding his wife but not, apparently of feloniously wounding with intent to do grievous bodily harm. Mr Justice Charles comment was "the jury have found that if you cut your wife's throat you did not intend to do her grievous bodily harm. That is the way you have in Cornwall I suppose."

The jury again came under fire, when they suffered the lash of Mr Justice Avory's tongue. He aroused strong criticism because of the remarks he made at Bodmin Assizes when the jury found a prisoner not guilty. Addressing the prisoner he said, "You will be surprised to hear the jury say you are not guilty." "Thank you sir," replied the man. "Thank the jury, don't thank me," said the judge. Thereupon, the prisoner said he would like to thank the jury and to thank the solicitors who had helped him. "Thank you everybody but yourself," said Mr Justice Avory who then ordered the jury not to leave the court. "You may wait," he said, "and see how justice ought to be administered."

A troubled spirit on the Moor

In the year of 1844 Matthew Weeks was committed to Bodmin Gaol and hanged for the death of Charlotte Dymond.

It was a brutal crime, it was said to have been murder, without doubt it shocked a moorland community, but at the same time left many questions unanswered.

The young couple lived and worked on a farm within Davidstow parish, Bodmin Moor. Both were farm servants and it was well known that they were fond of each other. How strange then, when Charlotte's body came to be found with her throat slashed on the bank of a moorland stream, it should be Matthew who stood accused of murder.

It was late one Sunday afternoon in April when Charlotte and Matthew left the farm. On reaching the end of the farm track Matthew turned to follow the road to Halworthy and Charlotte to walk out across the moor. When she failed to return Matthew was questioned and as the days wore on, with no sightings, the pressures of the close society he lived in proved too much and he left. A search continued, yet it took nine days to find the body, close to Rough Tor Ford, a crossing place in regular use on the moor. That, in itself one would have to say was surprising.

Following investigations an inquest was held and the jury brought in their verdict that "Matthew Weeks, late of the parish, labourer, not having the fear of God in his eyes but moved and seduced by the instigation of the devil, on the 14th April in the year foresaid, with force and arms in the parish of Advent, in and upon the said Charlotte Dymond in peace of God of our said Lady, the Queen, then and there being feloniously wilfully and of malice afterthought, did make an assault." The verdict went on to accuse Matthew Weeks of murder, although he was not present or represented. A parish constable was sent to trace the now accused and brought him back from his sister's in Plymouth to stand trial at Bodmin Assizes in the August.

The day of the trial was long for it was nearly 10.30 in the evening when the Foreman of the Jury delivered their verdict. "We are of the opinion," he said "that the prisoner is guilty."

So he was found guilty, despite a spirited defence by his Council, Frederick Slade, who found many flaws in the prosecution evidence, but failed to convince the Jury. It now only remained for presiding judge, Sir John Patteson, a black cap placed on his head, to pronounce sentence and in doing so utter the words Matthew Weeks feared to hear. "You shall be taken from hence to the place you came and be hung by the neck until you are dead."

"Your body shall be buried within the precincts of the prison," Patteson started, but, before he could conclude with "May the Lord have mercy on your soul." Matthew was seen to collapse onto the bench, where he had been sitting since just after nine that morning.

The days leading up to an execution always produced a rich harvest with people pouring into the town. Tollgates, inns, shops, pedlars, ballad singers, everyone who had something to sell or something to tell found a willing audience. On the day of the execution, it was estimated that a crowd of 20,000 gathered in front of Bodmin Gaol and on the sloping ground which commanded a view of the drop. This abutted the Wadebridge Bodmin Railway, facing south.

As the clock struck twelve the huge crowd was hushed as Matthew Weeks was led to his execution. The payment to the executioner was £26 for Week's neck. He remained silent, no "last dying speech" was uttered from the scaffold. The bolts were withdrawn, the trap fell with an awful sound, breaking the deadly silence. The body then remained suspended over the gaol entrance outside the south wall for the usual time - an hour and one minute.

Perhaps that should be the end of a tragedy, but here I would recommend you obtain a copy of the book 'The Charlotte Dymond Murder' by Cornish Bard, Pat Munn, or visit the 'Courtroom Experience' at Shire Hall, Bodmin. You may perhaps question if justice was carried out and if the troubled spirit of Charlotte Dymond will ever be put to rest?

Rough Tor and the Charlotte Dymond Memorial

Savagery punished: jealous miner went stoically to the gallows for passionate crime: A Possessive Murderer.

It was a crime of passion, a crime that was brutal, vicious, savage to a degree, a crime that ended the life of 16 year old Emily Barnes Trevarthen Tredrea and also ended the life of 23 year old William Hampton on the gallows at Bodmin Gaol.

As a young man Hampton, like many Cornish miners, went to America and he successfully worked there for some time, but returned to the Duchy and his village St Erth in October 1907. There were no convenient lodgings for him with his own people and he went to live with the Tredrea family, continuing as their lodger until the date of the crime, May 2. 1908.

Emily Tredrea shared with many Cornish girls a womanliness in advance of her age, and when she passed her fifteenth year there seemed nothing very strange in the fact that she 'kept company' with one so much her senior as Hampton.

The parents of the girl, who had noted the growing attachment of the pair, consented to a tacit engagement between them. For some months things went very smoothly with them. William Hampton was a steady young man who eschewed alcohol and was generally looked upon as a decent fellow among the local community.

Whether jealousy – for which apparently there was not a shadow of basis - was the cause or not, the fact appears established that a month or so before May he developed flashes of violent temper accompanied with language unfit for the ears of a girl.

She resented his swearing and they quarrelled over it, with the result that she eventually confided in her mother that she could not tolerate his language and had decided to have no more to do with him. She said the same to girlfriends, but expressed fear of his passionate nature.

Mrs Tredrea had left the house to attend to Hampton's grandmother, leaving Emily standing by the kitchen table eating cake and drinking from a tea cup. It was not quite 8.30 in the evening.

The gruesome story of the awful tragedy can only be gleaned by confessions from the wretched author of it, added to the flashing impressions of a bewildered and terrified little boy who bore witness to the whole event.

Hampton admitted the girl said to him "I have given you up. I shall not go with you any more". It is hardly credible that was all that was said, but the murderer detailed no further conversation, and later at his trial was said to be beside himself and, in consequence, devoid of coherent recollection.

He said he sprang from the chair on which he had been seated, seized the girl by the throat, bore her to the ground and strangled her, though he also said he did not think she was dead.

Upstairs, young Willy Tredrea heard a scuffling and a strange noise, so terrifying that he crept out of bed, peered over the staircase and saw his sister on the floor. Hampton had one knee on her stomach, his hands around her throat and both thumbs pressed into her neck. The little fellow darted into the bedroom, partly dressed then dashed down the stairs and out of the house to bring back his mother. Hampton picked up the girl placing her in a wicker chair, muttered something about her having 'been sick' then left the house. Then realising the hopelessness of his position gave himself up.

At his trial a strong plea for the reduction of the charge to manslaughter on the grounds it was not premeditated and the murder was not wilfully intended was put to the jury. They returned the only possible verdict, but added a recommendation for mercy due to the age of the young man.

An appeal was lodged but was dismissed. A petition containing 3,000 signatures for royal clemency, was obtained, all to no avail. Hangmen, the brothers Pierrepoint, arrived in Bodmin overnight and proceeded quietly to the gaol where they took stock of the prisoner and also tested the gallows previously used eight years before.

F G Stone Collection

The Condemned Cell, Bodmin Gaol

During his incarceration at Bodmin, both before and after his conviction, he was a model prisoner, his constant companion was the Bible and on Sundays his pure tenor voice could be heard far and wide.

On Monday night he fell asleep later than usual and woke early, ate some plain breakfast, then listened with acute attention to the closing ministrations of the chaplain. When, about five minutes to eight, Thomas and Henry Pierrepoint came into the condemned cell, he stood up and passively allowed the buckle strap to be fixed around his arms, prior to stepping out on his last journey. He uttered no sound throughout.

Outside the weather was gloriously fine, the sun striking through what had been a heavy mist. A large crowd had gathered, mainly young men and women. As the time grew near there was a short move up the steep hill by the side of the gaol, near the wall of which it was known the gallows had been erected. All was now silent.

©WHJ

The unhappy man had to traverse 40 to 50 yards, going along a brief corridor, then over three steps, out into the sunlight and the yard, but with a dozen more to the place of execution. Hampton showed great fortitude, walking erect and firmly, without requiring any assistance from attendant warders. He was very pale, but betrayed no marked emotion.

The silence broke, the drawing of a lever distinctly heard by all immediately followed and was drowned in volume by the sound of banging as of a heavy door being slammed. William Hampton was dead, hanged by the neck, notices were posted on the massive gaol doors, the crowd slowly dispersed, the brothers Pierrepoint made ready to leave Bodmin.

The jury saw the body placed in a black rough-deal coffin which, after a 30 minute inquest and a short service, was placed in a grave prepared in a garden plot within the prison walls. A small cross of red roses and later a stone with the initials W H would indicate the spot.

The post had brought a letter to Hampton that morning. Normally the postman would not have arrived at the gaol until 8.15 am, but he altered his route so as to deliver the letter at 7.30 am. At that time however, the condemned man was earnestly engaged with the chaplain and the unopened letter went with him to the grave.

The brothers Pierrepoint would not return, for William Hampton at the age of 24 years was the last person to be hanged within the high walls of Bodmin Gaol on 20th July 1909 at 8am.

Stagecoach at the Tyn-y-Coed Hotel, Capel Curig, North Wales

The perils of early travel by stagecoach

It was just over two hundred years ago that the first stage coach was making an appearance in Cornwall. Our moors and valleys running across the Duchy had proved to be severe obstacles in communications with England. The sturdy pack horse carried the loads and any wheeled coach or cart was a novelty with the local population, but times they were a-changing.

1790 saw the first service leaving Exeter on alternate days at 3 am travelling via Bodmin to arrive at Falmouth, a distance of about one hundred miles, just before midnight, a jolting bone-aching twenty-one hours.

By 1816 the mail coaches were the kings of the road, subjected to tight schedules. At the sound of the approaching coach horn, toll gates were thrown open, and the inns alerted to have the fresh horses ready, for on average, only three minutes were allowed for the change over. I can only marvel at the breed of passenger who also only had the three minutes to attend the toilet, buy food and drink and be back on the coach and away. The headquarters of the mail coach at that time was the Royal Hotel, Bodmin, on the great mail coach road through Cornwall to Exeter, with changing stations for horses situated around seven miles apart. On leaving Falmouth's busy port with its great sailing ships, the packets, they changed at the Norway Hotel (Devoran), Royal Hotel (Truro), Falmouth Arms (Ladock), Indian Queen (Goss Moor), Victoria Inn (Roche), Royal Hotel (Bodmin), Jamaica Inn, (Bolventor), Kings Head (Five Lanes, Altarnun) and The White Hart (Launceston).

The mail coaches were built for speed, not for passenger comfort. They could carry nine passengers, but the inside seats were only three and a half feet wide and three feet four inches from seat to roof. You only travelled by mail coach when speed was of the greatest need. The horses were chosen with great care; only horses of equal stride were put together to increase speed and reduce coach swing, as at speed a swaying coach could easily overturn.

The arrival of the coaches meant great excitement, with the mail taking, on average, thirty hours from London, bringing the latest news from England and Europe and, of course, arriving from Falmouth, news from across the world.

Cornwall's county town would have rung to sounds of horses being quickly moved around, shouted questions, hustle-bustle, mail bags being exchanged, loved ones departing, loved ones returning, joy, sadness, all in that short time; and then the inn's customers returning and Bodmin resuming its slow pace of life once again as, echoing in the distance, the guard sounded the coaching horn as the coach approached Callywith Gate and onto Bodmin Moor.

The 1850s were the 'Indian Summer' before the coming of the railway from Plymouth. The Quicksilver coach reigned supreme, by far the fastest coach in Cornwall, which covered, after a change of horses at Halfway Inn, the three and a quarter miles to Glyn Bridge over the River Fowey in ten minutes: this was the fastest stretch in the whole of Cornwall, an average speed of sixteen miles per hour.

In times of severe weather it was not unknown for the guard to unhitch a horse and carry mail across Bodmin Moor, hence, I think, the old expression "her/his Majesty's mail must get through."

A number of the old coachmen were heavy drinkers, exposure to all winds and weathers and long hours took their toll. This spelt danger, one example being near Jamaica Inn. The guard, in desperation, removed the driver to the rear of the coach and took over himself. About to descend a steep hill he shouted to the driver "drag on" (brakes on), the driver in his befuddled state shouted back his agreement and did nothing. The arrival of a single horse indicated a calamity which, of course, it was with several seriously injured.

A report of an accident in 1812: "On Friday last, as the mail coach was passing over Polson Bridge, Launceston, one of the wheels came into contact with an angle in the wall and the coach overturned. There were four outside passengers on the coach; three of whom were thrown over the bridge with the fourth hanging by his hands on top of the wall until he was rescued by the guard. A Mr Williams of London, one of the passengers, had his right knee badly fractured and one of his ribs broken. A Portuguese gentleman received several wounds and contusions to his body. The third escaped with a slight wound on his knee. The coachman was seriously hurt and the guard slightly." Such were some of the perils of travellers in those not so long ago days.

1859 saw the completion of the railway from Plymouth to Truro and the end of an era. The driver, Sam Prior sadly took the 'Quicksilver' from Torpoint Ferry - Liskeard - Bodmin - Bugle - St Austell - Grampound - Truro - Falmouth. To the end they kept the reputation for speed and regularity summer and winter, but a new era was dawning - the GWR "God's Wonderful Railway."

Camel and Elephant headed the Train

In 1796 it was proposed to build a canal from the then port of Wadebridge to Dunmere, Bodmin, to convey sea sand for farmers to improve their land and enhance production. Although this venture failed to materialise, the building of a railway did and in 1834 at a cost of £35,000 the Bodmin and Wadebridge line with trains terminating at Wenford - this being the main line with a branch to Bodmin - came into operation. The principal backer of the enterprise, was Sir William Molesworth of Pencarrow, and among the shareholders were the secretary, Mr John Pethybridge (Manager of the East Cornwall Bank), Bodmin clerk, Mr John Wallis, solicitor of Market Street, Bodmin and Reverend John Wallis, Vicar of Bodmin.

The line, laid on granite sleepers, not only carried sea sand inland, but also a considerable quantity of coal for local mines, and granite from De Lank Quarry at St Breward.

Passengers were very much of a secondary interest, although they had the advantage that the train could be stopped and boarded at any point along the line, but having said that, the company created history in Britain by running the first rail excursion.

In 1836 engines Camel and Elephant headed a train from Wadebridge to Wenford and back - 24 miles conveying 800 passengers at one shilling (5p) each, thus unknowingly they anticipated Thomas Cook's first rail excursion by four years. A further excursion took place in 1840 to witness the public hanging of the Lightfoot brothers; the railway running alongside Bodmin Gaol enabling passengers to spectate, without leaving their seats.

Bodmin had two stations, Bodmin North (Southern Region) and Bodmin General (Western Region). The General opened in 1887 to Bodmin Road and connected to the Bodmin and Wadebridge at Boscarne Junction on September 3rd 1888, thus joining with a mainline after 54 years of isolation.

During the 1800s over 3,000 tons of granite per year were being carried from the De lank Quarries at St Breward via Wenford to Wadebridge for shipment to, amongst other places, Bishop Rock Lighthouse, Cork and most of London's bridges including at that time, Putney Bridge, but of course the main traffic over the years was china clay, pumped off the moor to Wenford Dries and then by rail to Fowey or Par docks.

During the Second World War the line was upgraded to take GWR passenger trains should the railway become impassable through Plymouth. In fact, only twice was this complicated route with its reversals at Bodmin Road,

Bodmin General, Wadebridge and Exeter St Davids used, one train being the Cornish Riviera. Also at that time a small armoured train was kept at Wadebridge.

1963 saw the last steam passenger workings over the line, below are two route times taken from that year's timetable: Ex Bodmin Road 7.50 am, Bodmin General 8.08 am arriving at Wadebridge 8.27 am. Ex Bodmin North 8.43 am, Dunmere Halt 8.47 am, Nanstallon Halt 8.50 am, Grogley Halt 8.54 am arriving at Wadebridge 9.02 am.

With the withdrawal of steam came revised timetables in 1964 with a shuttle service to Bodmin North from new wooden exchange platforms built at Boscarne. It was the beginning of the end.

The North Cornwall line closed October 1966 and Monday January 30th 1967 passenger services between Bodmin General, Bodmin North, Boscarne and Wadebridge closed. Freight was finally withdrawn and the line closed in 1983.

The Bodmin and Wadebridge was a solidly built and well-run undertaking which deserved a better fate, being the first steam operated railway in Cornwall, the first public railway south of a line from Liverpool to the Wash to be used by steam from its opening, a pioneer undertaking over three years before the first mainline Birmingham to Liverpool and Manchester and carried passengers four years before the first mainline out of London.

Clapham Railway Museum

This carriage, built in Wadebridge, originally had three First class compartments but by 1860 two had been changed to Second class. Third class was open wagons with gaps in the floor to let the rain out!

Today the Bodmin and Wenford Railway operate steam and diesel trains from Bodmin General to Bodmin Parkway and Boscarne, carrying nearly 50,000 passengers per year.

108

Nanstallon: memories still vivid of colourful past - rail gave villagers a lifeline in hard times

Village life has much altered today but we all have memories. For the village of Nanstallon flooding was sometimes a problem. Almost every winter the stream that runs at the foot of the hill in the village would burst its banks and flood Rose Cottage, the home of Mrs Hambly.

This yearly experience no doubt led her to being well supplied with necessary provisions so she could retreat to a bedroom of the house until the water subsided once more. Immediately across the road, until he retired in 1945, was the blacksmith's forge of Mr Carhart. This later became the garage of Mr Clarence Pinch, who found nails and horseshoes in his adjoining garden. He grew beautiful tomatoes and flowers, claiming it must be the iron in the soil, an organic connection, somewhere.

Before mains water was brought through, many of the villagers had their own supply of water with wells in their gardens and in the dry periods would go to the spring at Three Waters. In the 1920s the doctors from Bodmin considered the spring at Berry Lane to be the finest source of water around.

The local taxi service from Bodmin to Nanstallon was a pony and trap, right up until the 1940s, with the driver and passengers making their way down the literally "Stony Lane" into the village, the carbide lamps glowing dimly and branches of trees brushing the faces of the passengers. Every year until the mid fifties the village would hold a carnival, in which many of the adults and certainly all the children would take part.

The Carnival Queen and her attendants would be selected from the young ladies of the village. Festivities would carry through to the evening, when a dance would be held in the institute. The music would be supplied by Mr Coppin, who would travel from place to place with his van containing musical equipment and loud speakers.

Although an expanding community, sadly the village no longer holds a carnival, but I am sure many locals have happy memories of days gone by.

Of course the pony and trap taxi was not the only form of transport, as the railway certainly played its part in village life.

People would make their way to the village halt, crossing the 'Old Rattling Bridge' over the River Camel, The old ironwork bridge was made locally in Wadebridge by Oatey and Martyne; the rattling coming from the loose wooden planks. Speed and time were never that important and often someone would be late, the train would arrive at the halt, the signalman would spot the person hurrying along the road and inform the guard - the train would then wait until the latecomer was safely on board and only then, with a cloud of steam and smoke would it pull away. One dear old soul who was walking along the track on her way to Bodmin market was offered a lift by the engine driver who was about to pull off. "Oh no," she said "I've got to make haste," and bustled on down the track.

Before the war, rabbit was the staple diet for many and for one local man, now long retired and residing in Bodmin, the railway for him as a young man was a direct route to the butchers. He would set his gin traps late at night or early in the morning and on seeing engine smoke in the distance would make his way to the track at Grogley Halt. Here the train would stop, hampers were loaded on with the driver who, on arrival at Bodmin General station, completed the shunting of wagons and then saw to the hampers of rabbits. There would be as many as 40 rabbits in a hamper and he would send perhaps 5 or 6 hampers every week. With 20 or 30 rabbit catchers assembled at Bodmin General station, hundreds of fresh Cornish rabbits were sent on their way up country to the cities of England.

Mention must be made of the engine driver, Bill Tucker, who would collect groceries, take shoes to be mended and help the local people along the line in a variety of ways. Those days have gone, myxomatosis finished commercial rabbit catching and Dr Beeching axed the railway branch line. Both were equally devastating to rural life.

Wadebridge to Bodmin train on the approach to Polbrock Road bridge. Today the track bed is the popular Camel Trail.